"It's hard to imagine that in this seventh co-authored book, Lichtenberg, Lachmann, and Fosshage have managed to create a thoroughly fresh vision of the psychoanalytic engagement, distinct not only from what other contributors have brought to us, but also distinct from their own past writings. Presenting, as they themselves write, '... a new synthesis of motivation, development, nonlinear emotional influences, and relational aspects of the psychoanalytic process...' Lichtenberg, Lachmann, and Fosshage now move to an enhanced focus on lived experience, on what it feels like for the 'doer-doing' as he or she moves into relating, creating, living, and breathing. Their novel and expert focus on the nonverbal, their exquisite elaborations on affect-tone and ambiance, generate a new appreciation of what the trio have already brought to us in terms of motivation and development. For example, I call attention to the clinical and conceptual distinction they make between disappointment and disillusionment. And, as always, there is an abundance of beautifully rendered clinical material. In all, this is a fascinating volume. It is groundbreaking and truly interdisciplinary in the best sense of the term. I can only add: these three have done it again!"

Estelle Shane, PhD, Board Member and Training and Supervising
Analyst, Institute of Contemporary Psychoanalysis, Los Angeles

T0383395

An Experience-based Vision of Psychoanalytic Theory and Practice

An Experience-based Vision of Psychoanalytic Theory and Practice looks at each individual as a motivated doer doing, seeking, feeling, and intending, and relates development, sense of self, and identity to changes that are brought about in analytic psychotherapy.

Based on conceptualizing experience as it is lived from infancy throughout life, this book identifies three major pathways to development and applies Lichtenberg, Lachmann, and Fosshage's experience-based vision to psychoanalytic psychotherapy. Using detailed clinical narratives and vignettes, as well as organizational studies, the book takes up the distinction between a person's responding to a failure in achieving a goal with disappointment and seeking an alternative path, or with disillusion and a collapse in motivation.

From the variety of topics covered, the reader will get a broad overview of the experience-based analytic conception of motivation begun with Lichtenberg's seven motivational systems. This title will be of great interest to established psychoanalysts, as well as those training in psychoanalysis and clinical counselling psychology programs.

Joseph D. Lichtenberg, MD, Graduate Baltimore-Washington Psychoanalytic Institute, is Cofounder of the Institute for Psychotherapy and Psychoanalysis, Cofounder of *Psychoanalytic Inquiry*; and Editor-in-Chief of *Psychoanalytic Inquiry* and the *Psychoanalytic Inquiry* Book Series.

James L. Fosshage, PhD, is a Past President of IAPSP; Cofounder, Board Director, Faculty, and Supervisor, National Institute for the Psychotherapies (NYC); Founding Faculty, Institute for the Psychoanalytic Study of Subjectivity (NYC); Clinical Professor of Psychology, New York University Postdoctoral Program in Psychotherapy and Psychoanalysis.

Frank M. Lachmann, PhD, is a psychoanalyst and Founding Faculty of the Institute for the Psychoanalytic Study of Subjectivity, and is author or coauthor of more than 160 journal publications and books.

Joe Caruso is an author, business advisor, speaker, and an advisor to top leaders on individual and collective behavioral change.

Mor Shechory-Stahl, PhD, is a Clinical Psychologist; Lecturer in psychotherapy programs in Israel (Department of Psychology, Bar-Ilan University; Levinsky College of Education); practicing psychoanalytic psychotherapy in private practice; advisory board member of 'In-Between', a nonprofit that supports divorced families.

Psychoanalytic Inquiry Book Series
JOSEPH D. LICHTENBERG
Series Editor

Like its counterpart, *Psychoanalytic Inquiry: A Topical Journal for Mental Health Professionals*, the Psychoanalytic Inquiry Book Series presents a diversity of subjects within a diversity of approaches to those subjects. Under the editorship of Joseph Lichtenberg, in collaboration with Melvin Bornstein and the editorial board of *Psychoanalytic Inquiry*, the volumes in this series strike a balance between research, theory, and clinical application. We are honored to have published the works of various innovators in psychoanalysis, including Frank Lachmann, James Fosshage, Robert Stolorow, Donna Orange, Louis Sander, Léon Wurmser, James Grotstein, Joseph Jones, Doris Brothers, Fredric Busch, and Joseph Lichtenberg, among others.

The series includes books and monographs on mainline psychoanalytic topics, such as sexuality, narcissism, trauma, homosexuality, jealousy, envy, and varied aspects of analytic process and technique. In our efforts to broaden the field of analytic interest, the series has incorporated and embraced innovative discoveries in infant research, self psychology, intersubjectivity, motivational systems, affects as process, responses to cancer, borderline states, contextualism, postmodernism, attachment research and theory, medication, and mentalization. As further investigations in psychoanalysis come to fruition, we seek to present them in readable, easily comprehensible writing.

After more than 25 years, the core vision of this series remains the investigation, analysis and discussion of developments on the cutting edge of the psychoanalytic field, inspired by a boundless spirit of inquiry. A full list of all the titles available in the *Psychoanalytic Inquiry* Book Series is available at https://www.routledge.com/Psychoanalytic-Inquiry-Book-Series/book-series/LEAPIBS.

An Experience-based Vision of Psychoanalytic Theory and Practice

Joseph D. Lichtenberg,
James L. Fosshage, and
Frank M. Lachmann

with contributions
from Joe Caruso and
Mor Shechory-Stahl

Routledge
Taylor & Francis Group

LONDON AND NEW YORK

First published 2021
by Routledge
2 Park Square, Milton Park, Abingdon, Oxon OX14 4RN

and by Routledge
52 Vanderbilt Avenue, New York, NY 10017

Routledge is an imprint of the Taylor & Francis Group, an informa business

British Library Cataloguing-in-Publication Data
A catalogue record for this book is available from the British Library

Library of Congress Cataloging-in-Publication Data
A catalog record has been requested for this book

ISBN: 978-0-367-54350-1 (hbk)
ISBN: 978-0-367-54347-1 (pbk)
ISBN: 978-1-003-08885-1 (ebk)

Typeset in Times
by Newgen Publishing UK

Contents

1 Preview, historical perspective, and the plan of the book   1

2 The treatment of Eileen   62

3 The treatment of Samantha   76

Summary of Chapters 2 and 3   105

4 Disappointment and disillusion   108

Discussion   120

Index   *139*

Preview, historical perspective, and the plan of the book

Preview of main contributions to theory

In this book we present a new synthesis of motivation, development, non-linear emotional influences, and relational aspects of the psychoanalytic process: concepts central to an understanding of human experience. We draw on the research, observations, and theories of others, but believe the integration we arrive at, especially about the influence of an underlying affect tone on a person's disposition, choices, and expectations, provides a fresh approach to how a doer doing experiences his or her relationship; his or her interests, skills, learning, work, and ability to play and enjoy; and living in his or her body. Broadly speaking, our integration provides a new view of aspects of clinical experience and especially the role of working through on the ambiance that develops between analyst and analysand. We also delineate the distinction between disappointment and disillusion as a response to failure.

This book is a continuation of our exploration of motivation, development, identity, and the clinical application of our conceptions. Beginning in 1982 in *Psychoanalysis and Motivation*, we have presented a concept of motivational systems. Each system is a group of affects, intentions, and goals that dominate what an individual is experiencing at any and every given moment. Each of the seven motivational systems (attachment, caregiving, affiliation, regulation of physiological requirements, sensuality and sexuality, exploration and assertion of preferences, and aversive antagonism and withdrawal) self-organizes in infancy and continues to develop throughout each phase of life (Lichtenberg, Lachmann, and Fosshage, 1992, 1996, 2011). In this book we move from concepts of psychic structures to an emphasis on human experience as it is lived. By lived experience we refer to an individual's implicit and explicit feelings, sensations, intentions, goals, and sense of self that emerge from any external or internal event or change. Rather than instinctual drives, we suggest that experience indicates seeking is the fundamental motivational spark for the human capacity at all ages to be a doer doing, initiating and responding, activating and taking in. To seek is the basic spark that activates each pursuit of an affect, intention, and goal of a doer doing.

We identify three pathways for development: the pathway for human relatedness and intimacy; the pathway for mastering of the environment; and the pathway for a healthy body, physiological regulation, and a good mind–body connection. To this traditional "bottoms up" infant-to-adult view, we add a "top down" perspective giving development a circular pathway. We propose that, in early infancy, experience is largely holistic, combining affect, sensorimotor activity, cognition, and memory. From these early intersubjective experiences an affective tone develops that underlies what the infant is seeking at any time. The underlying tone ideally consists of diffuse generalized feelings reflective of affection and sensual pleasure; a sense of competence, power, and confidence; and a sense of having a regulated, functioning body and physical well-being. Later experience exerts a top-down influence that confirms, augments, or alters the affective tone. When seeking leads to intimacy, competence, and good health, or when treatment leads to understanding and adaptive change, a negative underlying affective hum may become more positive. In situations of chronic or acute stress or trauma, the underlying affect tone will tilt toward feelings of being unloved, inadequate, or sick or sickly. The breadth of the underlying affect tone and its role in the core sense of self and early memory is a major factor in each individual's disposition and general modes of presenting his or her self – his smile, her greeting, his posture, her serious concentration, the music in her voice, his contagious laugh or his slumping posture, her eye avoidance, his irritability, or her touchiness.

Neonates begin life seeking to discover what they want: a physiological necessity, a relationship, stimuli that arouse their interest. Via sensorimotor activity, they then seek how to get what they want. If obstacles exist, they seek the means to overcome them. Through reflection, older infants and children increasingly seek to discover the meaning of their desire by forming a nonverbal or verbal narrative that speaks to the purpose of their seeking, its link to their core sense of self, and the three broad pathways for development. Each development pathway utilizes aspects derived from the affects, intentions, and goals of seven motivational systems. The patterns of seeking that spark activation in each pathway are affected by changes in age, skills, and environmental and social contexts.

Older infants and children begin to explore the edges, ranges, and potential of existing patterns of seeking. Shifts in existing patterns may result in the expansion or restriction of what a doer doing is apt to initiate or take in, activate, or respond to. The trend to explore the unknown, mysterious, or presumed dangerous intensifies greatly in adolescence.

A significant feature of the first year of life is the categorizing of the infant's experience into motivational systems of intentions and goals in which the affects are specific. We postulate that as a result of adaptive seeking, in addition to specific affects, the infant forms a deep underlying memory in the core sense of self that captures three generalized affective states. These states are like an underlying theme, an atmosphere, a hum, a matrix of affect tonality that sensitizes the doer doing to his or her particular affect rhythm of being and seeking. In adaptive development, the first deep emotional state is based on the emergence of a generalized state of affection, of positive interpersonal experience. The second builds toward a deep sense of the degree to which the infant has experienced the power to seek and accomplish learning skills, a mastery of tasks, and a spirit of inquiry and play – a broad general sense of "can do." The third reflects the infant's capacity to live in and with her body – a core sense of body self drawn from the activity of the autonomic system, the sensory apparatus, and sensorimotor activity including mirror neurons. The underlying sense of basic affection, power, and bodily well-being and the positive sensibilities that derive from it have a profound impact on identity, disposition, expectations, and the reciprocal interplay of any intersubjective experience. When present, a deep conviction of "I can love and be loved, and I have confidence in my agency, my 'I can do,' and my body's functioning, strength, and health and appearance" provides a gyroscopic stabilizer at times of stress and failure. When poorly formed or altered by more severe trauma, the effect on identity and seeking constitute central areas requiring therapeutic focus.

The psychoanalytic method is comprised of different components, each contributing to amelioration of emotional illness. Central is the associative/interpretive process leading to insight and meaning. The success of the exploratory approach is made possible by the relationship of an analysand being with a reliable, trustworthy, caring analyst skilled in empathic listening. Along with professionalism, the analyst must reveal herself to be involved personally in the give-and-take of transference/countertransference. To these two generally cited components of insight and an explicit relationship, we add the nonverbal, presymbolic ambiance between analyst and analysand that forms and alters over time. This unique aspect of analysis extended over time – this "working through" of generalized implicit feeling-tone experience – will impact and alter the underlying affect tone, leading to improvement in disposition and sensibilities. The analysand's underlying affect tone and the analysand–analyst ambiance are similar in that both are nonsymbolic affect tonal states, pervasive atmospheres, that reflect generalized experiences of relatedness, mastery and a sense of power, and bodily well-being.

The success of carrying forward an intention and goal by a doer doing leads to positive expectations and a positive propulsion, while failure may activate disappointment and a seeking of alternative opportunities to achieve one's intention – what we refer to as "resilience." However, if the emotional response is disillusion rather than disappointment, a collapse of intention rather than seeking results. In Chapter 4 we will present many clinical examples of disillusion.

An historic perspective (JL)

Growing out of the Enlightenment, psychoanalysis has been deeply concerned with both human experience and its transformations into creativity, and scientific explanation drawn from research and logic. Personal inclination and political necessity led Freud to tilt toward science. The clinical setting became the laboratory for observation and science-based research on psychic functioning leading to "metapsychological" formulations in experience-distant metaphors. The distinction between science borrowings for theory and experience-near case histories can be observed in Freud's borrowings from science for theoretical constructs (psychic structures, instinctual drives, id, ego, and superego) and the more accessible descriptive language of his case histories. First, "the unconscious" received its conceptual explanation in the topographic theory. Here the goal was to make the unconscious conscious, to convert primary process into secondary process. Dreams were the paradigm for unraveling condensation, displacement, and symbolization in order to discover a disguised desire and intention. Then, conflict, drive, executive and defensive functioning, and morality and ethics were accounted for in the complex idioms

of the structural hypothesis. This is the version of psychoanalytic thinking that brilliant scholars like Hartmann, Kris, and Loewenstein brought
to the USA as "ego psychology." Their disciples Brenner, Arlow, Wangh,
and Beres visited the local institutes to be certain the intricacies of ego
psychology were understood and taught, and aggressive drive was given
proper emphasis along with sexual drive. This was the period of my training, early practice, teaching, and writing: 1957–1970. I fully enjoyed
teaching ego psychology – the economy, logic, and fit of the pieces. It
reminded me of my love of trigonometry, where each part could be juggled
to make a fit in an equation. This "fit" proved to be a problem that became
exposed by the psychologists of the Rapaport-Klein Study Group. Ego
psychology was a closed system – each element was explained by another.
A wonderful intellectual exercise, but an experience-distant set of points
of view: the dynamic, economic, structural, and genetic.

Then in the 1970s I discovered Kohut's explanations that moved toward
more relevant clinical proposals about 'self' or, as I prefer, sense of self
or experiential self (Lichtenberg, 1973). Kohut's more experience-near
formulations about narcissism were far reaching; his adherence to some
structural terms like selfobject was less so (Lichtenberg, 1991). Rather
than an experience or *sense* of self, Kohut used the metaphor of a structure
that could be fragmented. Responses from significant others were regarded
as filling deficits in regulation – so the self was completed by taking in
needed capacities from the object to form a cohesive selfobject. The term
selfobject also came to refer to a necessary and empathic person rather
than an experience that led to feeling vitalized or soothed and comforted.

Research on infants provided a rich, new viewpoint and vocabulary for
development: Winnicott (1965) being alone in the presence of another;
Bowlby (1988) seeking a secure base at a time of danger and loss; Stern
in a *Diary of a Baby* (1990), using concepts of vitality, attunement, and
cross-modal sensory activation; and Beebe and Lachmann's (2002) viola-
tion of expectations. As I reviewed the wonderful accumulation of research
on infancy, I recognized that Hartmann's having added a fifth point of
view – the adaptive – helped to introduce a valuable link to an experiential
view of development. The adaptive point of view brought analytic theory
into direct contact with the experience of relating to both the animate and
inanimate world – a challenge that gives human experience its affirma-
tive coloration and direction. Adapting brings into focus an infant's initiatives and responses to both other humans (intersubjectivity), the inanimate

world (interaction), and his bodily needs. The individual's contribution to the intersubjectivity and interaction is to seek – to reach out with an intention, a goal, and an affect.

Experience – or lived experience, in our usage – refers to all the moment-to-moment occurrences that impact a person and all the implicit and explicit discrete and underlying emotions, intentions, and goals that emerge. Some of the continuous flood of information and sensation impacting each human will be in awareness, symbolic, and open to reflection. Other impacts are more subliminal, subsymbolic, and sometimes unformulated, but have an influence on behavior, intentions, and expectations. By centering on experience, we examine the impact of any event or happening emanating from the environment, the body, and/or the implicit or explicit memory of previous lived experience.

A word on our language choice. Referring to *experience,* we primarily describe feelings, vitality, enlivenment, narrative, gesture, thoughts, sensations, memory, expectations, fantasy, intuition, imagination, attitudes, intentions, and goals. Our point of focus is on the **sense** of self (not self-structure). Referring to activity of the *brain,* we refer to the right and left hemispheres, cortex, neurons, networks, and processes. Referring to the *mind,* we use experience-near concepts such as systems, pathways, self and object representations, RIGS, cataloging, differentiating, and adaptation. Bucci's (1957) theory of symbolic processes of verbal or nonverbal language and imagery, subsymbolic processes of visceral and autonomic sensory, and motor responses and their linking can elucidate sense of self and brain, as well as mind.

The book is divided into four chapters. In each of the four chapters we relate development, seeking, sense of self, and identity to changes that are brought about in analytic psychotherapy. In addition to the explicit benefits of interpretation and insight, we emphasize the implicit changes that occur in the ambiance between the analysand and analyst. We suggest that subtle affect alteration in ambiance is instrumental over time in changes in the underlying affect tone of the analysand. The underlying affect tone comprises three qualities of experience that are more generalized and atmospheric than discrete emotions: openness to affectionate warmth, having a sense of agentic power, and living in one's body. The generalized senses of affection, power, and bodily well-being are experienced as an underlying "hum" or sensibility. Once formed, the underlying experience of caring conveys the sense that the person has the hedonic tone necessary to give and receive affection, has a sense of having the power necessary to be effective as a doer doing, initiating and activating, and is a vibrant physical being. Caring, power, and bodily well-being provide an abiding feeling state that contributes to the individual's sense that life is worth living or, if deficient or lost, detracts from it. We see the foundational experience for affectionate caring as having an integral connection with sensuality conceived in its broadest sense from a mother's and baby's affection for each other to the tender goodbye of love ones to a dying parent. The fundamental experience of having power is derived from recognition and implementation of the infant doer doing's spontaneous seeking and intentional exploration of the inanimate world. The underlying feeling of bodily well-being emerges from forming a good mind–body connection that facilitates the regulation of physiological requirements.

We present our expansion of motivational systems theory in four related new conceptions. First, *seeking* is the spark that triggers the feeling, intentions, and goal of each activated motivational system. Second, from a development perspective, *three broad pathways for seeking* organize: the pathway for human relatedness and intimacy, the pathway for mastery of the environment, and the pathway for a healthy body and a good mind–body connection. Each of the three developmental pathways utilized one or more motivational system(s) in the intentions and goals being sought. Third, an *underlying generalized affect tone* emerges that reflects the adaptive success or failure of each pathway. Fourth, during successful analytic therapy, along with interpretation and insight, changes occur in the *ambiance between analyst and analysand* that relate to and are affected by the underlying affect tone. The modification of negative underlying affect tone is an integral requirement for analytic success. Fifth, the *effect of scolding and shaming on the intensity of seeking* and on identity is discussed.

In Chapter 2 we use a clinical narrative to identify positive changes in identity. By identity we mean the experience of who we are, as reflected in the narratives that emanate from a core sense of self as a doer doing. Narratives of identity emerge from who the person regards him or herself to be, who others regard him or her to be, and some combination of the two. In the words of Phillip Roth, "one's story isn't a skin to be shed – it's inescapable, one's body and blood. You go on pumping it out until you die, the story veined with the themes of your life" (Roth, 2013, p. 107). In our prior studies of identity, we considered how humans are able to maintain a high degree of constancy in their core sense of self regardless of many transitions of life and vicissitudes of adaptation. We used the theory of fractals as a fundamental form of broad explanation, and the reflections about past, immediate present, and future intentions of the wandering mind to explain consistency of identity and the narratives that exemplify it. In contrast, here we take up positive changes in identity emerging from analysis. Via a clinical example we illustrate positive changes in identity brought about by the combination of interpretation and insight, alteration over time in analyst/analysand ambiance, and moderation of the underlying affect tone.

In Chapter 3 we present a clinical example, with an emphasis on the profound role of seeking as it emerges in psychoanalysis. To seek for a particular experience, one that arouses interest and has a sense of purpose, is the propelling urgency that activates each motivational system toward its goal. Bowlby (1973) addressed the fundamental role of seeking in his axiomatic statement that the infant seeks a secure base at times of danger and loss. Kohut (1971) emphasized the infant's (and adult's) seeking mirroring affirmation, twinship belonging, and the enlivenment of idealization. In the clinical situation, how does the analysand shift seeking from what he wants and needs directed at the analyst, to changes in himself and/or the eternal world? Is seeking blunted by resignation to a negative expectation? How is seeking reflected in the therapeutic ambiance and in positive change in the underlying affect tone?

In Chapter 4 we present a case study and many clinical examples of disillusion and the collapse of seeking. In contrast to disappointment that leads to seeking alternative means to carry out one's intentions and achieve one's goals, disillusion often results in abandoning seeking and a temporary or lasting disruption of treatment.

First: seeking: its role as spark for motivational activation

The fundamental launching point (motivational source) for experience

Seeking is the spark for everything we do, feel, think, and imagine. In other words, seeking is the spark for our individual and collective humanity. Seeking provides the means by which each individual develops and forms, maintains, and alters his or her capacities, his or her unique identity. Seeking through reflection is the means by which we create a daily and lifelong sense of complex meanings as we experience our lives together and separately. Our study of seven motivational systems points to seeking as the impetus activating the affects, intention, and goals of each motivational pursuit. The primary role of seeking can be immediately recognized when our focus is on an individual's experience and in addition receives strong support from contemporary brain research (Alcaro and Panksepp, 2011). Shifting our focus to experience and seeking as the primary source of motivation shifts our verbal presentation from language borrowed from nonexperiential sources (psychic structure, neutralized energy) to a language of experience.

In *Portnoy's Complaint*, Philip Roth refers to his character Alex Portnoy's reason for his compulsive masturbation. Alex is turned on to sex with a girl by her "nice ass," or "tits and nipples," or ability to suck, but some disappointing failure on her part triggers another round of masturbation – as do episodes of severe frustration with his mother and father. So what does he want? He wants sexual excitement, orgasmic relief, release from the severe tension of frustration, disappointment, humiliation, and anger. Or we can ask: what does he seek? He seeks sexual excitement, orgasmic relief, release from the severe tension of frustration, disappointment, humiliation, and anger. When the source of being a doer doing is body sensation (sensual arousal, pain, need to urinate and/or defecate, shortness of breath, hunger, thirst, repellent odors, and other emotion-laden states), *I want* and *I seek* seem indistinguishable as triggers for action. But when an infant scans the room with no specific desire or goal and discovers moving shadows that catch his attention, seeking is a primary motivational impetus that leads to exploration and discovery of what he wants to look at.

Seeking stimuli

The neonate, from birth on, is biologically primed to seek stimuli. A very young infant held in the feeding position interrupts his feeding to roll his eyes up to gaze at his mother's face about 8 inches away (Stern, 1977). She responds automatically to his heightened alertness and speaks to him in a higher pitched rhythmical tone. His arms begin to move in a rhythm synchronous to her speech. As she turns away and prepares to resume feeding, he signals with his eyes for a repeat contact "run." She responds and then resumes feeding.

Another example of seeking occurs when a toy on a string is dangled in an area 10 to 12 inches in the midline before a neonate. Everything about him changes. He fixes his eyes on it, his pupils dilating. His whole body goes into immediate motion. His fingers, toes, and mouth point toward the object; his shoulders hunch forward. At a slightly older age, he will instantly swing his arm toward the object, his fingers contracting to a grasping position. He may miss contact with it, his arm overshooting the toy by a wide margin. He makes three more attempts, coming closer each time, until on the fourth he hits the toy and reacts with excitement (Trevarthen, 1977).

When examined with stop-frame photography, the building up of a total body-response pattern can be observed to occur in a regular rhythm of four times a minute, in which each incident of total concentrated attention is followed by a collapse and a further buildup. The whole sequence is characterized by the jerky movements of all the body parts. If a familiar person enters the infant's perceptual field, everything about the baby will soften. The same sequence of buildup and collapse of body movements toward the mother occurs (fingers, toes, mouth, dilated eyes), but the movements are soft and smooth, with the mother entering into a "courting dance" of rhythmic coos, eye and mouth movements (also at the rate of four times a minute) (Brazelton, 1980).

These examples indicate that the mother–infant dyad functions so that the infant is capable of organizing and reacting to perceptual input by action responses. The infant's perceptual preferences are givens, e.g., preferences for specific visual configurations (Bower, 1971; Carpenter, 1974) and auditory ranges (Condon and Sander, 1972; Terhune, 1979). From the beginning, perception consists of an active organizing of stimuli. It is guided by inborn preferences and primed by the impelling urge to seek both animate and inanimate objects.

The action responses are in turn differentially patterned depending on whether the activities are *with* humans or activities *on* nonhuman objects:

> The contrast of the infant's behavior and attention span when he was interacting with his mother, rather than an inanimate object, was striking as early as 4 weeks of age ... one could indeed tell from looking at

a toe or a finger whether the infant was in an interaction with an object or a parent – and by 4 weeks of age, even which parent it was.

(Brazelton and Als, 1979, pp. 357–359)

Mothers will approach their babies to help collect or contain them. They will smoothly reach around their baby's body and support him, or they will make eye contact or voice contact to engage the baby's attention and regulate the stimulation level. Fathers commonly approach their babies in ways that heighten stimulation. They may engage in games of poking or playful grabbing. Their talk to the baby may be rhythmic, but the pace is usually faster, the voice louder and more staccato. In diapering, mothers will gently lift the baby by his buttocks, slide the diaper in, and smooth the baby over as the process is completed. Fathers commonly pick the baby up by his legs, shove the diaper under, and let the baby plop down onto the table. By 3 weeks, babies talked to from behind by mother show the smoothing controlled response. When the father's voice is heard the baby will respond with a jerky excitement. Each parent thus becomes a partner in a feedback loop pattern according to expected mutual responses.

The infant is capable of participating in increasingly complex affective behavioral communications. The infant does more than receive, delight in, or react against the communications of his caretakers. He actively signals his preferences in order to stimulate responses (Moss and Robson, 1968). The process of being regulated by verbal and nonverbal communications from the caretaker and furnishing cues to the caretaker is a reciprocal exchange from birth on. In the earliest neonate period, the baby "communicates" readiness to seek interaction as a property of the active wakeful state. The mother must furnish the correct reciprocal feedback to capture the baby in eye-to-eye contact (or, in a blind baby, in auditory contact). Even though adultomorphized, the mother's often-stated conviction that her baby is looking at *her* carries with it the seeds of the remarkably rapid sense of a recognition response. By 7 to 10 days the mother can count on consistent eye-to-eye contact, and the baby is building up a response pattern of shared regularity. By 4 weeks, the cues from the baby are often sufficiently clear that the mother can sense the infant's readiness to prolong the state of playful interactive attentiveness. Utilizing the readiness to seek, the mother and baby gradually expand the contact runs, until by 3 months these have become conversational "games" (Stern, 1977). Communications having more formal characteristics normally develop at about 4 to 5 months. At this time the infant undergoes a general expansion of his whole state of alertness, probably associated with neurophysiological maturation and reorganization. The infant can be depended on to give much clearer signals of his preference to seek initiation and termination of the play activity. It is now that the mother's sensitivity to the infant's initiation of variances begins the process of self-selective making of choices on the part of the child.

Looked at this way, body-language signaling, nonverbal vocalizing, verbal signal comprehension, and verbalizing are an unbroken, additive developmental sequence (Bruner and Sherwood, 1980; Call, 1980). Experienced largely holistically, this sequence leads on the one hand to an increasing discreteness and precision of exchange between caregiver and child, while on the other hand it leads away from the unique bond of intimacy that is quickly established holistically between infant and mother. The dancelike synchrony of the initial behavioral communications provides the substructure for the deepest levels of empathic contact and hedonic tone which underlie the relatively more distinct and discursive exchanges that characterize most verbal communications (Stern, 1977).

Four related processes of seeking

First, seeking combines the impetus and means by which the individual *identifies* his wants, needs, and desires. A person's successfully seeking his desires and needs experiences a flicker of interest and a change in internal state that leads to recognition of here is who or what I want.

Second, seeking combines the impetus and means by which an individual *formulates intrinsic or explicit plans* to obtain what she wants and to *overcome obstacles* if present. Seeking to form a plan to obtain one's desire is experienced as the person being a doer doing, sometimes alone in the presence of the other, often while interacting with someone experienced as a helper or hinderer.

Third, seeking is the impetus for a person's *reflecting to discern the meaning* of who or what he wants, obtains, or fails to get. Seeking in this instance is to understand the effect of the success or failure of the doer doing on the person's state of mind, adaptation, expectations, sense of self, and identity. Seeking to discern the meaning of one's needs and wants involves interest, reflection, and a spirit of inquiry, often building to a lasting curiosity that touches on identity.

Fourth, seeking is the spark for each individual's variably intense inclination to explore the edge of the known, the sanctioned, and/or the prohibited. Seeking to test limits, throwing caution to the winds, may be motivated by a desire for heightened experiences of exhilaration or detachment, defiance and/or indulgence, the chaos of a drug high, sadistic episodes of inflicting pain or sexual dominance, and masochistic states of fear, pain, or sexual submission. Seeking the edge may be manifest as behavior and/or in fantasies where no limits may curtail the enactment. Depending on the nature of the testing behavior or fantasy, the result may be moments of enhancing enlivenment with feelings of liberation. Or, in some sadomasochistic or sociopathic testing of limits, the result may be harmful to the self and others (pathological). Or, in some experimental testing of limits, the result may be innovative and creative.

In *Neuroscience and Biobehavioral Reviews*, Alcaro and Panksepp (2011) establish seeking as a fundamental motivational dynamic of the brain.

> Appetitive motivation and incentive states are essential functions sustained by a common emotional brain process, the SEEKING disposition, which drives explorative and approach behaviors, sustains goal-directed activity, promotes anticipatory cognitions, and evokes feelings of positive excitement which control reward-learning. All such functions are orchestrated by the same "archetypical" neural process, activated in ancient subcortical areas and transported to the forebrain by the mesolimbic dopamine (ML-DA) system. … These patterns may be considered basic "SEEKING" neurodynamic impulses which represent the primary-process exploratory disposition getting integrated with information relative to the external and the internal environment.
>
> (p.1805)

Winnicott's experiment on seeking

An experiment of Winnicott (1941) illustrates an example of adaptive seeking. Infants aged 3 to 13 months are placed in a set situation that challenges the infant to cope with uncertainty and anxiety. The baby is positioned in her mother's lap so that she can reach for an attractive mouthing spatula. The mother is instructed to focus her attention on Winnicott and not engage or interfere with the infant. The baby reaches for the spatula, hesitates, and looks at Winnicott and her mother with big eyes. (Blocked from any seeking of affectionate interaction with her mother, the infant's first seeking is to gain the sensual mouth pleasure from sucking the spatula and with it a sense of power resulting from carrying out an intention to grasp and play with an object of her desire. The second seeking is to resolve a learned inhibition against touch and grasping by seeking guidance and affirmation of her intention from mentors.) The infant may wait with her body still, withdraw, or bury her head in her mother's blouse. (The third seeking is to find a means to pull back from and contain her conflicted intention "I want it but I don't know if I should grab it." The infant who buries her head in her mother's blouse also seeks to gain comfort for her anxiety through activating an attachment experience.) Gradually saliva begins to flow in her mouth, and before long her body movements become freer and she puts the spatula in her mouth. The infant's body enters the struggle, adding an intensity to the call for the infant to exert her power. Winnicott regarded the transition from anxiety and hesitation to daring to act on desire as a reliable indicator of a valuable increase in self-confidence. (The fourth seeking involves implicit self-reflective awareness of the autonomic nervous system activation [salivating], and a mounting sense of determination to act, a restoration of a sense of power.) Now the baby regards the spatula as belonging to her. She bangs it on the table and then drops it, introducing a you-pick-up-I-drop game. (The final seeking is to explore the inherent possibilities of the object for play.) Winnicott states that

> little steps in the solution of the problem come in the everyday life of the infant and young child, and every time the problem is solved something is added to the child's general stability and the foundation of emotional development is strengthened.
>
> (p. 245)

We emphasize the role of seeking in solving the problem of overcoming paralyzed initiative and becoming a restored doer doing, an augmentation of the sense of power of the experiential self.

Seeking and motivational systems: what desired adaptive experiences are sought in each motivational system?

The affect, intention, and goal that delineates each of the seven motivational systems involves a definable human desire or need: a desire for an attachment, an affiliation, and being a caregiver, a desire to explore and assert preferences and experience competence in the use of one's capacities, a need to express aversion and regulate bodily needs, and a desire for sensual pleasure and sexual excitement. While the "I want" varies greatly in the intentions and goals of each motivational system, *seeking* is the fundamental experience present in the pursuit of what is wanted in each system. To seek is an omnipresent active or potentially active experience – including at night (as evidenced in dreams). But the intensity of seeking varies for each motivation system at any given age, context, or time.

Through our study of motivational systems, we have identified seven groupings of experience that infants, children, adolescents, and adults seek consistently with one another, dominating the path to awareness at any moment. Each motivational system becomes manifest as an affect, intention, and goal. Each of the three pathways to development involves several motivational systems. The experiences sought are

1. closeness, trust, and affection for and with another person (attachment motivational system)
2. having a connection with and belonging to a group – family, peers, team, country (affiliative motivational system)
3. responding to the needs of another with caring, concern, compassion, and altruistic behavior (caregiving motivational system)
4. being comfortably physiologically regulated, having physical health and strength and a good connection between mind and body (motivational system for the regulation of physiological requirements)
5. being efficient, skilled, and confident in mastery over the environment, being able to learn, work, and play (exploratory-assertive motivational system)
6. when encountering a situation felt to be aversive, being able to regulate conflictual seeking and intending by being able to withdraw to safety or oppose effectively (aversive motivational system)
7. being able to find and enjoy the pleasure of sensual vitality and/or soothing with others or alone, and to find pathways for orgasmic excitement and relief (sensual-sexual motivational system).

In *The Clinical Exchange* (Lichtenberg, Lachmann, and Fosshage, 1996), analyst and analysand have to explore and understand the unfolding of their individual and mutual seeking. How free or inhibited, how recognized, or repressed, or denied, how compatible with other goals is the analysand's seeking in general or in a particular instance? How does seeking influence expectations? Does the successful fulfillment of expectations lead seeking to intensify? Does the failure of expectations to be fulfilled lead to resignation and apathy? How do we work analytically with analysands who tend not to seek? Or with those who seek to derive all they desire not from their life outside their analysis but from the personal responses of the analyst and the treatment itself?

While we regard seeking as omnipresent, the influence of seeking on the experience of being an involved doer doing varies greatly. We can speak of this as the person having turned off to seeking in a particular context, or never having turned on, as with some autistic children who have never been turned on to seeking face-to-face emotional exchanges. When turned on, seeking activates interest ranging from a flicker to a sustained involvement based on deep curiosity. The expectations that emerge from past experience influence the direction and intensity of seeking. The rewards and stir of interest from positive experiences activate seeking for their repetition and easily expand to related intentions and goals. Negative experiences exert different influences on seeking. The negative influences that the individual is able to cope with and overcome lead to an optimistic belief that he will be effective in his seeking for solutions to obstacles presented by comparable negative experiences. Seeking solutions to negative experiences and disrupted activities and relationships increases in likelihood when a person's interest is strong and when she has a sense that there is an adaptive purpose to the struggle. Negative experiences that are overwhelming or where efforts to overcome lead to repeated failures result in avoidance or aversion to seeking, and experiences of feeling powerless, pessimistic, resigned, and defeated. Alcaro and Panksepp (2011) state that "in depression seeking is reduced, while in addictions seeking is reorganized to focus on ultra-specific appetitive memories and compulsive activities." In each experience, the actual or experienced presence or absence of others and the role they play as helper or hinderer will give a strong relational turn to seeking.

We can regard the source of negative experiences as emerging from opposition, hindering, demands for submission, being terrified, shamed, or humiliated. But another source is the absence of needed contexts for positive experience to emerge. Self psychology pointed to the absence of empathic responses of affirmation, commonality, the uplift of admiration, sponsoring, and mentoring. For the full adaptive development of affect, intentions, and goals in each motivational system particular relational, cultural, and physical contexts and provisions are essential. We have proposed that resilience is illustrated when a person actively seeks a needed experience that, implicitly or explicitly, he recognizes to be missing (Lichtenberg, Lachmann, and Fosshage, 2017).

Seeking and then what? The intersubjective influence

Seeking may elicit a wide variety of responses from a caregiver. Each frequently repeated response will have a profound effect on immediate outcomes, the nature of attachment, and the development of expectations.

A child's seeking may be recognized, supported, enhanced, and often shared. This response contributes to a secure attachment. When the child's seeking is at times recognized and supported, and, at other times unpredictably not recognized, ignored, or rejected, the result is an ambivalent insecure attachment. Or, when the child's seeking is not repetitively recognized, ignored, rejected, angrily opposed, or responded to with scolding and shaming, the result is avoidant attachment. Or, when the child's seeking is repeatedly unrecognized or, if recognized, insensitively overridden by the parent in a fashion that sets up a persistent angry, frustrating relatedness, the result is an avoidant and/or disorganized attachment.

A factor that has received little investigation is the varied effect of the caregiver's warning that a child's seeking and moving forward with a particular intention and goal may place the child in danger. When the child is able to recognize the risk and danger intuitively, or when it is explained and understood, belief in the validity of the warning becomes a component of the child's reality and the parent is regarded as a reliable source to look to for guidance. Alternatively, the child's own experience or observations and the persuasion of others may lead the child to question the validity of the supposed danger. The child may conform in his behavior since maintaining his parent's love and approval would seem to him a better resolution than testing the veracity of the warning. Or a child may safely challenge the proposed risk, which enhances or overvalues his judgment in comparison to authorities.

We are suggesting that a child grows up forced to draw conclusions about the validity of authorities, and the parent's appraisals about risk are important in the effort to know what is "true."

Second: three developmental pathways for seeking

The developmental pathway for seeking human relatedness and intimacy

From their experience in the intrauterine environment, neonates bring a differential recognition of their mother's voice, a pattern of sucking to self-soothe, and body movements to move away from noxious stimulation. They are responsive to a human face, preferentially to the eyes and mouth areas, and to the human voice, with a heightened reactivity to higher pitch and especially to prosody and musicality. Their 10-12-inch visual focal point concentrates gaze, attention, and interest on the sphere of mother–infant feeding, holding, and social interchange, and then gradually expands with a comparable expansion of interest to the broader environment. Along with vision, auditory, and kinesthetic interactions, their heightened sensitivity to their mother's smell contributes to a strong discriminating recognition. In addition, they are predisposed to recognize, respond to, and be affected by the emotions of their caregivers. When distressed and disrupted, they respond to a caregiver's comforting with the restoration of a calm state and a return of the ability to activate interest.

They readily initiate a high percentage of interactions with a caregiver. These frequent initiatives (Winnicott's spontaneous gestures) give the caregiver an opportunity to recognize, affirm, and validate the infant's budding agency, his/her affects, intention, and goals. For the infant, this experience coheres into a sense of self as a doer doing with others. They respond to a stimulus presented in one or more sensory modes both in that mode and in alternate (cross) modes as well. They imitate and mimic observed movements and gestures.

By the end of the first year, well-adapted infants have acquired from their face-to-face interactions with a caregiver an integrated package of:

1. knowing how to read cues about the affects and intentions of others, the affects and intentions of themselves as a doer doing, and the reciprocal interplay of dyadic affects and intentions – the foundation for empathy,

mentalization, a theory of mind, and a secure base at a time of danger and loss

2. a warmth of greeting, a means of showing affection, of lighting up at the sight of a loved one

3. the cues of how to carry on a conversation – first nonverbal, later verbal with all the subtlety of stops, pauses, and starts coordinated with the affect-laden prosody and musicality of speech

4. the beginning affect-laden narrative of identity: who the infant is in the mirror of the caregiver, who the caregiver is in the interaction with the infant, and what affective ambiance they create between them – the emotional vitality of their intimacy, the foundation for creating imaginative characters and dramas in mind wandering and play sequences

5. patterns of behavior based on each's attentiveness to the intentions and goals of the other, coordinated with the caregiver's guiding the infant's intentions through mirroring, approval, and redirection – thereby providing the foundation of the infant doer's socialization.

A child's or adult's capacity for intimacy emerges from an aggregate of developmental experiences: 1. Knowing the interplay between the emotions and intentions of others and his or her own, 2. Being able to converse through affectively rich subtle verbal and nonverbal means, 3. Having a creatively rich imagination, and 4. Being able to socialize with an expanding range of contacts.

Attachment

Neonates are prepared by evolution to respond to faces. They will look at a drawing that has an outline of facial features and not to a drawing in which the same abstracted features of two eyes, nose, and mouth are randomly placed. From their experience in utero, with the sound of her voice heard externally and vibrating internally, her smell, and rhythms, neonates are prepared to respond differentially to their biological mother's whole being. Infants experience their mothers not as bits and pieces of stimuli – a sound plus a sight that they have to put together laboriously – but as an integrated whole (Stern's cross-model sensory experience, 1985). The nature of this integrated whole is interactional: that is, mother the speaker (her articulating face, her vocalizations, her movements, and her affect) forms a category – a narrative that is coordinated with the infant's responses, vocalizations, affect, movements, and mimicry (Lichtenberg, 1989b). The same innate responsiveness that creates this early experience of attachment (bonding) with the biological mother enables infants to form a similar differential response to any persistent maternal caregiver (maternal in function, not necessarily in gender). The affective quality that solidifies the path to attachment is being and feeling safe in the hands of a caring other (Winnicott's holding environment, 1965). The emotion-laden sense that "I am safe with you" plus the affects and sensual feelings stirred by mirroring affirmations become integrated as a nonverbal imagistic story of her and my face, her and my sounds, her and my touch, her and my body, her and my rhythms, and, by three months, her and my smile.

Communication From the first cry to the calming of distress in a feeding to the folding into the receptive arms of a caregiver, neonates and mothers convey information that each requires to be optimally responsive to the other. The caregiver's success in picking up and responding to the nonverbal narratives of the infant's needs and intentions facilitates the formation and functioning of the attachment, sensual, aversive, and exploratory motivational systems. Verbal communication – major achievements for all humans – is not necessary to form and tell a story to oneself and others. Dogs are wonderful communicators of their stories "I love you," "Take me out," "I'm angry or hurt," "I do (or don't) want to be with you": all this told by body movement, bark, head gesture, eye movement, and focus. And dogs understand the meanings of human verbal communication about both emotions and intentions. So dogs and infants do not need words to form and tell stories of I like, I don't like, I want, I don't want, I look toward, I look away. Infants can and do form images that tell meaningful stories to themselves and others – as do humans all their lives in dreams, mind wandering, reveries, fantasies, and artistic creations. But without words human life, as with people with mutism, is barren in relatedness and communication both with others and to oneself. Humans evolved language, and especially conversational language, to bind people in groups enabling the enjoyment of commonality and kinship. "Motherese," with its musical higher pitch, begins at birth as a caregiver's engaging chatter to her baby.

Each language has its own basic elements of speech, pronunciation, and musicality: its vowels, glides, timbre, and pitch contours; its pre-voice and delayed voice onset time; its timing cued to turn taking and opening to response. Infants who are read to while in utero from a Dr. Seuss book evidence recognition of the sound pattern after birth (DeCasper and Fifer,

1980). Recognition only occurs for the particular Seuss book read to them. This means that by birth, infants can distinguish phonological contrasts. Normal infants are innately responsive to any language or languages they hear daily. This responsiveness applies to any language humans have created anywhere in the world. The universal responsiveness to any known language does not last. At 12 months and after, infants can no longer automatically pick up any language they had not been exposed to. This suggests that infants in the first year are restrictively sensitive to the nuances of languages spoken to and around them by people from whom they are seeking safety, mirroring, and twinship commonality.

When exposed to synthetic sounds that are not found in any human language, six-month-old infants who could detect vowel changes readily in their native language to responded differently: "They could neither differentiate automatically nor be trained to in spite of rewarding" (Lichtenberg, 1989b, p.74; also Eimas et al., 1971). Thus, picking up and responding to speech and the nonverbal early stories it tells is innate. The two experiences – attachment and communication – are intimately entwined and interdependent. Words have no meaning for an infant without face-to-face coordination, sharing of affects, chatter and vocalizing, and all the other early caregiver–baby interactions. All these interactions are experienced holistically rather than as separate happenings. Meaning comes from the arousal of interest by the impact of recognizing and sharing affects, intentions, and a goal. A feeding, a shared look, a burping, a look around the room all involve an affect, an intention, and a purpose. Communication, in the form of maternal commentary and infant babbling and vocalizing, provides an undramatic but indispensable accompaniment to what the two doers are doing with each other. Not until relatively recently have early attachment and communication been recognized as necessary precursors for the older infant to become verbal and conservational (Lichtenberg and Thielst, 2018).

The developmental pathway for seeking mastery of the environment, confidence, and competence

Neonates seek and respond with interest to changes in the environment such as light, sound, and movement. They recognize the contrast between a recurrent familiar experience and a novel stimulus and establish a new category. They recognize contingencies guided by innate biases and affectively charged values, especially the contingencies that involve help-ful or hindering responses to their intentions and goals. They seek and respond appreciatively to being helped to deal with desires activated in mastery of the nonhuman environment.

While the pathway for the development of human relatedness (the attachment, affiliative, caregiving, and sensual-sexual motivational sys-tems) begins with recognition of and responsiveness to the human face and the musicality of the human voice, the pathway to the development of mastery of the environment begins with the recognition of and respon-siveness to an object, a thing (dolls, spoons, toys, stuffed animals) (the exploratory-assertive motivational system). Face recognition and object recognition occur in different areas of the brain (the fusiform gyrus for the face, the interior temporal gyrus for the object (Schulz et al., 2000; Klin et al., 2003).

For an infant, an object – say, a rattle – plays a different role in her emo-tional state than a face. Sarah doesn't want to get into her infant seat and begins to fuss and thrash about (the aversive motivational system). Sarah's mother tries to comfort her, with no effect. Then her mother shakes a rat-tle before her eyes; Sarah focuses on the rattle and its sound and instantly calms – a complete shift in her mental state: in her affect, intention, and goal. The infant's mother's effort to force her into the infant seat resulted in a disruption of their attachment experience and a shift into an aversive state. What did the rattle do? The rattle captured Sarah's interest – interest being an affect state that when fully activated can engage the entire focus of the sense of self (the exploratory-assertive motivational system).

A particularly important developmental advance in the experience of mastery and enhancement of the sense of self transpires from the complex functioning that emerges from the interplay of existing lower-level subcor-tical and cortical functioning and the maturation of higher-level cortical capacities. This change brings about reflective functioning and the diver-sity of more ordered narratives, played out with blocks and Lego, math problems, music skills, and stories from books and TV.

Regulation and power

Each child emerges from infancy with a sense of being able to self-regulate in respect of particular affects, intentions, and goals while need-ing help from caregivers in other motivational endeavors. And each child will have an implicit recognition of whether the benefit of his regulation accrues to him, to the caregiver-regulator, or to both. The more he senses implicitly that it benefits both him and the caregiver, the more he can feel pride in his power to control his impulses and to please others. To decide to act or refrain from acting conveys a purposefulness that is power in a positive sense in comparison to the power of opposition – of thwarting the unwelcome imposition from others. Thus, the "no" in gesture and the "no" in words at the end of the first year (Spitz, 1957) – the "no" so necessary for regulation – may convey to the self (and to others) a sense of power: when I self-regulate and I don't hit or bite, grab or drop, gobble down, or mess up, I can feel pride in my power and in my being judged to be a good boy, as reflected in mother's and father's faces. Alternatively, when I become oppositional and antagonistic or turn away and withdraw or explore and venture where I have been told not to, I feel a sense of power to negate and obstruct and an identity as uncontrolled and uncontrollable, obstinate and rebellious, and a sense of shame along with the power. Three factors contribute to an infant's sense of adaptive power, both as applied to specific intentions and to an underlying feeing state of the sense of self. First is the parent's recognition and affirmation of the infant's self-activated initiatives. Second is the infant's recognition of a sense of purpose both for when her initiative is supported and when it is diverted. Third is the sense for the infant of the caregiver as helper rather than hinderer.

The "yes" and "no" of regulation in infancy takes on a number of forms that distinguish the types of attachment. Secure attachment involves positive self and self-with-other regulation. The infant is confident of his safety and a flow of affection, whether being helped or playing alone in the presence of the other (Winnicott, 1958). Ambivalent attachment involves a regulated attentional focus in which the infant is preoccupied with whether she is being accepted or rejected. Based on the mother–child interplay, the infants alternatively reach for and push away when being held and play with a toy while keeping a watchful eye on their mother. Avoidant attachment involves the infant's aversive oppositional regulatory stance. They turn fully away from the mother with complete attention to their toy. And the one-year-old who evidences a disorganized attachment demonstrates a severe problem in regulation both in relating and playing. Each form of attachment affects the underlying sense of power to be effective or ineffective in the world of human relatedness and mastery of the environment.

During infancy, body physiological regulation is a central focus for caregiver and child. Physiological regulation is based on the ability of both mother and infant to pick up and coordinate signals. For an infant, sensations tell him when he is hungry or full, needs to urinate and/or defecate, breathe more easily, drift off to sleep, relieve stomach gas, have a bumped or scratched knee soothed. The caregiver needs to recognize and respond to the infant's communicative signal of the need or distress within a reasonable span of time. This leads to an integrated sequence of signals: sensation and external indicator, recognition (which cry means what?), and timely response. When as a result of the caregiver's recognition and ministrations the child's negative sensations abate, the infant builds an implicit sense of "my mother gets me, and we make an effective pair." And at a sensorimotor level, I know my body: when I'm restless and want to move, when I'm tired and want to stop, what itches and needs to be scratched, when I feel good and when I don't. The successful integration of physiological patterns and relational themes constitutes effective regulation. Success in regulation can originate either when an infant signals to his caregiver who then responds to him, or when a caregiver anticipates the infant's need. With further development, regulation is increasingly the child's own. The sense of context for regulation shifts between caregiver and infant and infant on her own, but a sense of the body, its comfort or distress, is a constant. Much emotion is generated in the doing of successful regulating: The baby experiences relief and appreciative love. The mother often experiences a struggle to recognize and puzzle out what and how she is being called on to activate or respond to, and how is her devotion to caregiving (her "primary maternal preoccupation"; Winnicott, 1956) to be balanced with her other interests and activities without resentment. Positive and negative emotions stirred in the early regulatory interactions remain throughout life and can emerge whenever there is a call for physiological self-regulation.

Parents provide mobiles, rattles, toys, and stuffed animals to respond to and activate their infants' interest, curiosity, and seeking. Nature offers changing light and shadow, sounds like rain and thunder. Pets move about and lick. For the infant, the interest stirred by these attractors contributes to the enlivening of the sense of self and presents a challenge to the mother–child interaction. Does the caregiver recognize and support and/or sensitively modify the child's spontaneous flow of interest and the seeking that goes with it? Recognition alone conveys a form of sharing. Recognition and facilitating or modifying adds a coloration to sharing: the sense of the caregiver as a helper. Not recognizing when the child needs assistance to support her interest, or ignoring the child's intentions, or overriding it with the parents own, triggers a sense of the other as hinderer. Three-month-old infants make a definitive distinction between a helper and a hinderer and the emotion stirred by each (Hamlin et al., 2007, 2010).

Significant principles of regulation are required for a child to learn to play safely and enjoyably, and to develop the skills needed to master the challenges of her environment: don't run out into the street, glass will shatter, walls are not to draw on, shoe laces must be tied, toys must be shared when friends come over. When the infant's emerging interests and intentions to seek and explore and test limits are recognized, guided, and helped, and a positive affect aroused, the skills that form and the regulations that guide their usage will be comfortably internalized. With respect to the core sense of self, the regulating of seeking builds a fundamental sense of power: "I can do." When an infant's emerging seeking, interests and intentions are repeatedly ignored and abandoned, or opposed and overridden, efforts to regulate will be responded to with rejection, obstinacy, and rebellion.

When adaptive, the underlying affective sense of positive, trusting, affectionate relatedness and of power as a doer doing, whether formulated at a given moment or not, will often be apparent to others. The readiness of a smile, the easy openness to the overtures of others, the gestural communication of "let's be an 'us' as well as a 'you' and 'me' " easily influence an accessible other toward friendliness and friendship. Power feels and looks different. Power is conveyed by the forcefulness of presence. John enters the circle and immediately the others make way for him. Kate joins a planning group and her friends say "Glad you're here. We are stuck, and we know you can help." While the underlying sense of caring trends toward friendship, trust, and intimacy, the underlying sense of power trends toward being reliable, having good judgment, and evincing a capacity for leadership.

The regulation of the sensual-sexual motivational system is focused mainly on the older child's seeking for sexual arousal. During infancy, finger sucking, body rubbing, and genital fondling may be restricted based on cultural mores. Shaming is the parent's main weapon against culturally sanctioned self-arousal – less so if an activity like finger sucking is viewed as helpful self-soothing. Shaming, along with guilt, may be used to prohibit any behavior viewed as bad. For the Oedipal-aged child, fear of retaliation from a parental rival (castration anxiety) along with shame and humiliation are the central barriers to sexual excitement (Lichtenberg, 2008).

The developmental pathway for seeking a healthy body, physiological regulation, a pleasing appearance, and good body–mind communication.

Neonates have a largely unrestricted pathway from body sensations of all types to psychic affective arousal. For an older infant or child, the immediacy of the mental experience of body sensation gradually becomes more regulated so that body sensations are less commonly dominant factors in ordinary consciousness. Neonates begin life with a cheek reflex to turn their head to find and begin to suck on a nipple to reduce hunger sensation and experience fullness and relief. From the coordination between a body sensation that signals a physiological need and the caregiver's response (the motivational system for the regulation of physiological requirements), infants get the cues they need to signal others and themselves about hunger, thirst, a stuffed-up nose, sleep, urination, defecation, needing exercise or rest, having discomfort or pain, as well as a general sense of bodily well-being or a dystonic state. Since messages in the form of sensation are continuously flowing between body and mind, each infant, child, and adult must learn which signal to attend and act on, and which to ignore or suppress without negative consequences – the foundation of physiological regulation and physical well-being.

Building on their exquisite sensitivity to temporal features in the environment, regularity, duration, and rhythm, infants develop a sense of familiarity with the repetition of events – such as the rhythm of feeding, being put to sleep, being put on a potty. These experiences are then categorized, remembered with an affective tonality, and become a powerful source of guidance and orientation.

The mind–body connection

Body involvement in one or another sensorimotor form is an accompaniment to the emergence of an emotional experience. Anger involves muscle tension, frowning, and clenched fists; fear involves movement away, eyes dilated, and face tense; shame/humiliation involves eyes turned down, body and head slumping; affection involves facial smile, body upright, eyes wide, lips curved up; pride involves postural straightening, head up, smile; excitement involves muscles tense, eyes alert. These affective experiences are triggered by an event or happening, actual, remembered, or fantasized. Perception, cognition, affect, and sensorimotor activity emerge as a unit – the body activity is a component of the whole.

The mind–body connections that originate from body sensations turn on a body signal of varied intensity. When the intensity reaches a particular threshold, the signal receives cognitive attention and a call for action. Toilet training involves getting the child to recognize intensifying body sensations in the abdomen and bladder and take socialized measures for relief. Hunger, thirst, and elimination all have gradients of intensity so that the timing of recognition of the signal for the rising sensation will differ for the individual – sometimes to the detriment of having a needed response. In anorexia and obesity, the mind hijacks the pattern, rendering meaningless the clues from the sensations.

Pain also varies in intensity but leads to the activation of attention at low intensities, and, at high intensity, dominates psychic functioning. Alternatively, the psychic goal of experiencing power, thrill, and success in rivalry can motivate the individual to participate in rough physical sports or risk-taking exploits regardless of the likelihood of bruising, falls, broken limbs, or concussion.

When confronted with protracted pain, bodily trauma, and painful interactions, infants tend to form a category of aversiveness and antagonism, rage and hatred and/or avoidance, fear, and disdain. The response pattern leading to intimacy often becomes rigidly and painfully aversive, leading to a psychic wall of avoidance, or, worse, self-inflicted pain and indifference to the pain of others.

Pain makes a person dislike a body part, or his whole body. He would want to get away from it if he could. Sensual pleasure makes a person like his body. It feels so good he wants more of it, seeks the feeling state sometimes at the risk of censure. Sensual pleasure may be heightened during a massage, back rub, or gentle stroking of the genitals. Less intense sensual pleasure may be built into many ordinary activities, like a breeze on one's face when walking or riding a bicycle, applying cream to a body part, eating leisurely and savoring the food, hearing music, looking at an attractive person. We believe that a person who emerges from infancy with underlying positive affect tone based on sensuality will seek and respond to both the subtle and overt opportunities for sensual pleasures in daily life – both interpersonal and body centered. Similarly, a person who emerges from infancy with an underlying positive core sense of self is able to use his sensorimotor capacities to carry out intentions in play, and will seek and respond to opportunities to exert his will in a variety of challenges.

Sensuality as the glue that holds together the infant's human relatedness and body sensations

An infant's love affair – her sensual core experience – is with her mother's smiling face, tender holding, kisses and hugs, gentle cleaning of her body, feeding, drifting off to sleep with a lullaby, and the musicality of mother's voice. Freud identified sexuality (not sensuality) as having origins in the erotogenic zones (zones of heightened stimulation and pleasurable sensation) of mouth, anus, and genital – all potential participant organs in an adult's orgasmic experience. Sucking her fingers is certainly a sensual experience, as is being sung and read to, bathed, hugged, fondled, kissed, rocked, or the air on her skin as a diaper is removed. One or another of these experiences occurs in one or another of the shifting states from alertness to sleep. Their repetition provides a continuity of hedonic experience that oscillates with distress and returns with relief from the distress. While sensual experiences emerge largely from baby–caregiver interplay and secondarily as a product of self-soothing or rocking, the older infant becomes the creative organizer of a complex form of sensuality in his play with a transitional object.

An infant's use of a blanket as a transitional object (Winnicott, 1953) illustrates the role of sensuality in creating a hedonic tone. A blanket is selected for its sensual properties: its texture and warmth, absorbing of smells, and ability to be molded against any part of the body. The blanket's otherness lends itself to representing or replacing the comforting other – but a comforting other that is under the command of the self. A blanket's otherness also facilitates its being imagined as a reliably available playmate and friend. Along with its otherness, the blanket also represents an extension of the self when it is carried about or cried into. The balance between qualities of discrete emotions and the generalized feeling states that emerge from an infant's experience with her "blankie" tilts heavily toward a pleasurable affective tone. The blanket experience has great power for its user since the child as doer both activates the state of comfort and companionship and takes in what she has activated in her imagination.

We propose that sensuality plays a role in the development of empathy. As an infant senses that his sensual delight in pleasurable interplay with his caregivers is shared by them, he gets his first recognition that you and I are alike – we have something in common (Kohut's twinship experience, 1971). Added to the sharing of affection is the recognition through mirror neuron activity that when you reach for me lovingly it is the same as when I reach for you lovingly. The combination tells the young child "I can sense both your affect and your intention" – the fundamental properties of the empathic mode of perception (Lichtenberg, 1981). Empathic sensing of this nature both derives from sensual interplay and adds to sensual enlivenment. But what occurs in the inevitably frequent experience of shared negative feelings and intentions? The same process of sensing into the state of mind of another – seeking to understand her negative feeling of anger and fear, with an intention to punish or reject – informs the child of another aspect of commonality: her own primary or reactive negativity. An attribution that the child is angry and wants to punish, dominate, or destroy, is fearful or sad and wants to run away, hide, cry and mope can originate from the self-appraisal, the appraisal of the other, or both. A child can come to accept some negative attributions with a degree of openness to acknowledge and rectify. Some attributions about self or others with whom the child is involved lie beyond recognition of their validity, and at times even lie beyond imagination. When this degree of negativity prevails, a positive trend toward empathy that had begun with intersubjective sensual pleasure encoded as an underlying affectionate affective tone can activate a capacity for compassion – a great stretch when confronted with evil.

Two modes of experience: 1) holistic and 2) linear

The distinct processing by the left and right cerebral hemispheres has been well documented (Schore, 1994). The left hemisphere functions through analytic cognition, logic, reasoned reflection, and verbal and number skills leading to complexities of language, math, and science. The right hemisphere functions through holistic cognition, intuition, imagination, reverie, and a heightened responsiveness to sensory stimuli: music, art, the beauty of nature.

A paper honoring Professor Traugott (2017), (see Lichtenberg and Thielst, 2018) describes an experiment on individuals who have acquired both a native and a later-learned language. The exclusion of the right hemisphere with unilateral shock therapy stimulated the patient to speak the learned language. When the left hemisphere was excluded the patient could speak only his native language (Perani et al., 1996*)*.

Acquiring a native language in infancy and acquiring a later-learned language are two different experiences. Learning a language after infancy requires a step-by-step task of mastering its words, grammar, pronunciation, and idioms – a laborious experience of purposeful doing. In contrast, hearing mother's speech with its musicality, engaging in face-to-face exchanges, making mouth movements, babbling, vocalizing, sounding "mmm" and saying "Momma" is a continuous flow of integrated doings that we experienced more as a turning on than a manifestation of a planned intention. The infant's smile turns on when the musculature and brain mature and flows immediately into the existing face-to-face emotional communication. Similarly, crawling, pulling up and standing, and walking all turn on when the musculature is ready. The turning on of these capacities contributes to the neonate's and infant's experiences as a doer doing in the world, interacting with caregivers or alone in their presence (Winnicott, 1941).

During the period of turning on to intersubjective experience, the infant responds to any repeated activity by categorizing elements of the experience – mother, father, feeding, diapering, going to sleep, awakening – and draws distinctions between the categories. What is familiar is distinguished from what is novel and the somewhat novel activates interest and curiosity, while too much novel is a turn off.

A three-month-old infant is exposed to two scenes. In the first scene, a figure with googly eyes receives a push up from a helper that is needed to succeed in an intention to mount an incline. In a second scene, the figure is pushed down by a hinderer, and thus falls down the incline. The three-month-old is able to distinguish between the happenings in the two scenes. When then exposed to the helper and the hinderer, the infant responds differently. He looks at the helper while eye-averting from the hinderer (and at 5 months reaches for the helper) (Hamlin et al., 2007, 2010).

The point we wish to emphasize is that all these developmental advances and turn ons in the first year occur in the highly emotional context of infant–caregiver intersubjective experience. We regard each turn on or turn off as a sequence of happenings, of now-moments, each flowing into the next. Each experience involves an emotion-laden combination of human relatedness, body sensation, and agency that is experienced holistically.

In comparison, much (but not all) later conceptual, emotional, and behavioral sequences are experienced as temporally and contextually discrete and subject to reflection. So, seeking attachment, opening to regulation, implicitly learning to communicate, experiencing both specific emotions, and underlying generalized affective tones of attention and power come together as a turn on that is more unitary and integrated than discrete and linear.

Critical patterns of the neonate and young infant's experience that contribute to the three pathways and an underlying affect tone

Freud first proposed sexuality, and later the dual drives of sexuality (libido) and aggression (death instinct), as humankind's essential motivations. He regarded the neonate as living in an oceanic state until recognition of reliance on a caregiver for basic needs awakened the infant to the presence of others. Other influential views of early infancy are Mahler's concept of an undifferentiated state, and Klein's paranoid schizoid position dominated by projective identification.

We offer a different view of the neonate's and young infant's state and the essentials of their motivation. Our view focuses on the neonate developing an attachment to a primary caregiver concurrent with forms of regulation and modes of communication. Together, attachment, regulation, and communications provide a foundation for the three developmental pathways in seeking. Success or failure in the development of each pathway activates a generalized underlying affect tone of affection, competence, power, and bodily well-being. The interrelated developments of attachment, regulation, and communication are experienced in nonverbal, largely sensorimotor narratives: "You are there for me"; "I calm or enliven in sync with what you do with and for me"; "We get each other, and I get better at getting you to get me"; "I have the ability and power to carry out many of my intentions"; "I am a doer doing – seeking, exploring, playing, arranging, and rearranging, crawling, standing up";

> From all we do together, and I do alone, I experience lots of different discrete emotions, but, in addition, I experience a more generalized underlying affective state – a tone, a hum, my sense that the world and my doing in it stirs emotion in me.

The underlying affect tone derives from each of the three pathways for development: a sense of affection – of loving and being loved; a sense of the power derived from successful agency; and a sense of bodily well-being.

Underlying affect tone

It has long been known that infants are affected by the feeling state of those around them. Maternal post-partum depression results in the child and adult being vulnerable to some form of dysphoria. The enveloping affect state of the sadness of a house in mourning, or the fear state of warfare or other traumas such as the anxiousness commonly experienced by a child of a holocaust survivor, predispose many individuals to a vulnerability to emotional disturbances. In contrast to these inescapable generalizing influences on affect tone, in ordinary experience the affects associated with the intentions and goals of each motivational system and the narratives that give meaning to them are relatively specific to the intentions and goals of the system: attachment and affiliation – safety, affirmation, commonality, affection, joy, admiration; physiologic regulation – sensations of discomfort and relief; exploration and assertion of preferences – interest, efficacy, and confidence; caregiving – altruism, and concern; aversive – fear, panic, anger, rage, hatred, shame, humiliation, disdain, domination, and submission; sensual-sexual – pleasurable sensations, erotic arousal, and excitement.

Regarding affective experience as either an enveloping predisposition or a series of specific emotions associated with particular intentions and goals fails to recognize the significance of an underlying affect tone and a sense of power as a doer doing. In ordinary healthy adaptive development, the sense of self as it emerges from infancy has an underlying abiding hum of an affective tonality and that sensual (not sexual) experience is largely responsible for its quality. The sensuality to which I am referring includes the up-beat experience of face-to-face greeting, smiles, playful hide and seek, mimicking, the musicality of an upper-pitched maternal voice, the tender caress of being held, the arousal in tickle and tease play, the thrill of being held up high by Daddy or riding on his shoulders, and the titillation of doing something forbidden and getting away with it. And sensuality includes the pleasurable experience of calming and soothing, being rocked and gently petted, and drifting off to sleep with a lullaby and reading from *Goodnight Moon*. In contrast, the sense of power as a doer doing derives from success in carrying forward intentions and goals, of competence in initiating, responding, activating, and taking in needed information and skills. The sense of power communicates to others as a presence – a mental and physical force to be reckoned with. Being warm, caring, and inviting, and being a rigorous, strong presence, are not in themselves gendered traits. Girls and boys, women and men, have a full range of possible intensities of inviting warmth, power, and competence. How the underlying hum from infancy will develop in gendered forms will be determined by the culture in which the girl or boy grows up.

The repetition of positive experiences during recurring daily states of infancy builds expectations and confidence. The positive experiences stimulate nonverbal stories of being a doer doing both when interacting with caregivers and when alone watching a mobile, shaking a rattle, playing with toys, and self-soothing with a blanket. The confidence that in future endeavors these positive expectations will come to fruition is the source of an underlying attitude of optimism and the affect tone that accompanies it. The optimistic attitude includes the implicit belief that being both loved and loving will be present or, if lost, will be restored. The affect tone of loving and being loved and that tasks will be mastered and skills expanded originates directly from the infant's personal intersubjective experience with his caretakers. But the infant's lived experience includes awareness of the shifting emotions and atmospheric affects in his surround that don't directly involve him personally. That humans are born sensitive to affects in their surround is supported by the finding of contagion in the nursery when otherwise comfortable neonates will cry if they hear another cry. Do the parents work together well and lovingly? Do they have the ability to overcome obstacles? Or is their relationship one of domination/submission, with all the resentment that accompanies it? Are the parents generally disorganized, unable to plan and function together? Do they subject each other to the corrosive effect of contempt and disdain? These disturbances in the parent's relationship with each other make it particularly difficult for a child to successfully meet Oedipal period challenges. In later life, children raised in situations of parental discord often carry a vulnerability to failure in their attempts to form intimate relationships based on a fundamental sense of goodwill. In contrast, infants and children who experience a positive intersubjective ambiance in their surround develop a deep implicit sense that in intersubjective exchanges goodwill generally prevails, or, if lost, will be restored.

Those fortunate infants whose deep underlying implicit memory is of mastering the self-regulation needed for comfortable socialization and mastered skills, and the joy of play and the confidence that they can influence others to help and participate with them in tasks that expand their agency, will as children and adults convey their internal conviction of power in their way of being "present" – a force to be reckoned with. The concurrently occurring experiences – attachment, communication, regulation, and the emergent underlying affect tone of affection and power – begin as an interaction in which the mother's internal preparedness interacts with the temperament and receptivity of the neonate. This mother–infant interchange creates the specific recognition and connection between this particular baby and this particular mother. They seek each other emotionally and physically. They communicate, telling each other stories: "You're my sweet little baby"; "Mother comes, smiles – nice"; "You are hungry"; "I greet your nipple with my sucking mouth." As they signal each other about their individual needs, feelings, intentions, purpose, and goals, they adjust their bodies and the pace and patterns of their mutual doings. With each doing – attachment, physiological regulation, interest, exploration, playing, teasing and joking, opposing or accepting, caressing or soothing – a feeling of the moment emerges and, along with it, a broader emotional sensibility – an ambiance that belongs to the dyad and remains fundamental for the affective dispositional state of infant, child, and adult. This property of emotional sensibility of the mother–infant or any other attached dyad underlies and bears close association to the pervading atmosphere – the ambiance – that emerges between analysand and analyst in the length period of "working through."

We use the term "disposition" to describe the overall repetitive attitude and sensibility of a person. Jane is lively and friendly. Her greeting is warm and inviting. Her smile elicits a smiling response. She is a pleasure to be with. At work she gets intensely involved and conveys competence and determination. Our postulate is that Jane is evidencing a predisposition derived from her earliest encounters with her caregivers and the many mastery activities of the first year. In contrast to Jane's immediately apparent affable friendliness, Sarah presents as a business-like force to be reckoned with – a doer doing exerting her sense of power over her task and her colleagues. In more relaxed moments, she is pleasantly sociable.

As we have stated, we believe these modes of being emerge from the development in the neonate and infant as an underlying generalized affect state – a hum of sensually desired affection and of a sensorimotor derived sense of the ability to carry out an intention and goal within an ambiance both serious and playful. These are the affective underpinnings of the experiences that result in positive attachment and a sense of mastery and the assertion of preferences. These foundational states are incorporated into the core sense of self as a generalized hum – a thread of affect tonality running along with moment-to-moment activity.

Jane's and Sarah's core sense of a hum of affection and power are the product of positive responsiveness to positive caregiving. Alternatively, the predisposition from the first year may be to depression, fearfulness, serious self-doubt, irritability, sensitivity to shame, or being seen as bad and oppositional. The variations of maladaptive affective experiences leading to forms of insecure attachment play a role in the matrix of the underlying affective tonality, leading to the predispositions to be sad, anxious, grumpy, easily provoked, and to be biased toward a negative evaluation to the seeking and activity of self.

We consider development in general and that which occurs in analysis as a circular process. Beginning with the seeking of the neonate and infant, each subsequent experience of affects, intentions, and goals is affected by expectations and predispositions derived from prior development – including the underlying affect tonal state. This is the bottom-up part of a circle. Increasingly with age, especially in adolescence, prior patterns are modified, enhanced, or defended against – this is the top-down part of the circle (see Alcaro and Panksepp, 2011 for a related concept). At the top is the highest level of narrative and meaning derived from reflection (Lichtenberg, Lachmann, and Fosshage, 2017). At the bottom is the underlying affect tonality of states of affection, agency, and body sensation. In between are all the stages on the pathways for development. An over-simplified rendering of the circle is that a well-loved, cared-for infant seeks comparable experiences in her warm greeting, friendly approach, and sensitive awareness of others. The warmth of her approach emerges from the affective tonality from which narratives about self and others, identity qualities, and behavioral patterns form. The successful experiences of the adult to offer and elicit friendship and closeness becomes a top-down enhancement to the underlying positive hum.

The concept of an underlying affect tonality gradually becoming increasingly representative of affection, power, and living comfortably in one's body helps us understand what is accomplished by "working through" in analytic therapy. In an effective therapeutic exchange, explicit and implicit experiences of seeking and the affects, intentions, and goals being sought are recognized and interpreted. With success in the inquiry about maladaptive seeking, the analysand is free to alter his or her feelings and intentions and become a more effective, proud, and confident doer doing in his treatment and daily life. As this process of "working through" extends over time, the recognition, interpretation, and understanding conveys a sense of accomplishment that translates to an increased pervasive sense of power. Each increase in capacity as a doer doing as a result of analysis adds a top-down increase to the analysand's confidence in having success as a seeker.

But what about the underlying generalized sense of affection, of being loveable and loving? This opens questions about analytic technique, especially the tradition of neutrality, anonymity, and abstinence and the common practice of long silence and formal manner in approach. The source in childhood of the patient's conflicts involving affection, sensuality, friendliness, affability, and warm, caring closeness may be recognized, interpreted, reflected on, and understood. This is a process of seeking to learn about – to make sense of, and, from that, gain a degree of power to move toward improvements in human relatedness; a top-down enhancing of the underlying sense of power to unravel inhibiting interpersonal experiences. The seeking that makes this analytic process possible will have roots in the predisposition emerging from the underlying hum of affection and sensuality but little impact on the enhancement of its positive influence. In response to what he incorrectly heard as a cold, affectionless response from his daughter Cordelia, Lear states "Nothing begets nothing." Analysis conducted without affect by a cold "objective" analyst – largely, but not entirely, a caricature – would beget no positive strengthening of the underlying affect tone of affection between the analyst and analysand; warmth and caring, friendliness, a timely response to distress are top-down contributions to a more foundational hum of being someone worthy of giving and receiving affection.

Stated differently, contemporary analytic therapies, especially self psychology and relational psychology, recognize the necessity for an intersubjective atmosphere of emotional sharing that mirrors and enhances the underlying tonality of something that begets the something that gives life a positive sensibility: the smile of "glad to see you," the handshake of "you're my friend," the hand of comfort on the shoulder, and even, with some analytic pairs, a hug.

In a post-analytic study, former analysands were asked what they remembered from their treatment that was helpful. One person answered "the day my analyst lent me an umbrella." This example stands for many instances of provision: adjusting hours or fees, a visit to the hospital for an ill patient, attending an art opening, comments on clothing, sharing a joke, engaging in a moment of playfulness that lightens and humanizes. Such provisions convey caring, adjustment to a particular context so that the main intention is promoted

Miss U, a teenager finishing high school, continued to be very distressed as the session ended. Having grown up in England, early on she introduced the ritual of a handshake before leaving. As we shook hands, JL intuitively sensed that she did not want to let my hand go and my left hand rose to enclose her hand. Our eyes met, with mine conveying my concern and compassion and hers conveying the meaning to her of my support.

For the older child and adult in daily life, and in analysis, an expectation that optimism and goodwill will prevail becomes a conscious, guiding, organizing principle that has a positive effect in bringing about confirmation. We are suggesting that a positive affective tone, belief in goodwill, and optimistic expectations emerge from loosely formulated holistic sensibilities. These sensibilities underlie the later affectively rich narratives that give expression to differing motivational states. But whether positive or negative, underlying generalized affect tonal states are not inert as sources of influence – they are active in their contribution to the ambiance that will emerge from every significant interpersonal relationship. Just as humans are highly susceptible to the effect of the ambiance of their personal interactions and their environmental surround, they are constant creators of an ambiance that develops between them and any significant other and any significant intention and goal in work and play.

To summarize: For ordinary adaptive development, the turn on to human relatedness requires a series of interlocking experiences all occurring in the same time period, with each experience enhancing the richness and efficacy of the other. As mother and infant offer their psychic readiness to join in creating a safe haven for nurture and affection, each needs to tell the other what's up and find out what the other is conveying. In words and actions, mothers tell their baby how he needs to be for her caregiving intention to succeed. And the baby, in his facial and body messages, tells his mother how she needs to be for him to be happy and relieved of distress. Thus, in one holistic "package," an infant and a mother learn to communicate with each other and regulate each other. And, along with their interpersonal communication, an infant learns to communicate with herself. And, along with the mutual recognition, the infant learns to regulate herself. And, from the emotions that are experienced as a result of success or failure during the relating, communicating, and regulating, the infant develops and experiences generalized, underlying, affective states of being or not being loved and loveable, of having or not having a sense of power to be an effective doer doing, that exerts a generalized positive or negative effect on moment-to-moment experience.

Two distinct processes are involved in a young infant's developing a deeply felt connection through attachments; learning to communicate emotions, needs, intentions, and goals; and engaging in mutual and self-regulation. One process responds to lived experience by forming differing categories of familiar, repeated, psychic events. These categories self-organize and self-stabilize into motivational systems. The categories exist in dialectic tension with other motivational systems, opening the way to shifts, enhancements, and reorganizations of intentions and goals. In contrast to the functional focus of this process that leads to increasing adaptive differentiation, another process tends toward a broadened integration and synthesis. In *Narrative and Meaning* (Lichtenberg, Lachmann, and Fosshage, 2017), we pointed to this process of expanding integration and synthesis as it applied to "master" narratives, generalized cultural and religious myths, the broad total effect of a great piece of music, and the emergence of a generalized sense of personal, family, and cultural identity. These examples all apply to the narrative themes and sensibilities of the motivational systems of an older child and adult. Returning to the infant in the first year, the integrative synthetic process involving attachment, communication, regulation, and affective tone, when adaptive, may originate in a particular sensory mode but easily spread across mode (Stern, 1985). Two generalizing lived experiences result. First, from the attachment connection, communication, regulation activity, and body awareness, feelings emerge leading to caregiver and infant each influencing how the other is experienced. An infant's turn on is not to his *attachment and communication and regulation and body sensation*; the infant's turn on is to each as it folds into and influences the other holistically. Second, a healthy adaptive core sense of self emerges from a sensually affective, centered mode of generalized pleasurable experience and a task-centered mode of confidence in having the power of agency and a body that is regulated and sensorially pleasurable. Emerging along with the broad sense of pleasurable experience is an optimistic belief in self and others, along with confidence that generally controversies will be resolved with goodwill in many, if not most, human relations. In addition, pleasurable experience and an underlying implicit hedonic tone will be activated by an aesthetic feel for the uplift from the beauty of the creations of nature and man. Even at its most consolidated, a positive tone of affection and/or power is subject to negative influence by physical illness, persistent stress, or acute trauma. But even when turned off, a positive sense of loving and doing as a central sensibility is a powerful resource for a turn on by treatment.

Components of the psychoanalytic process: the ambiance between analysand and analyst and the underlying affect tone

Recognition of the need to bring about positive change in a negative underlying affect tone helps to identify different processes inherent in psychoanalytic treatment. We commonly distinguish between the therapeutic effect of an exploratory associative interpretive focus and the relational aspects of analysis. The goals of free association, empathic understanding, and interpretation are to encourage a spirit of inquiry; help to bring into awareness feelings, intentions, and goals; recognize influences from childhood; discover meanings; and open the way to more adaptive choices. This exploratory aspect of the treatment employs primarily verbal, preverbal, and sensor-motor narratives. Affects are discrete and, to a degree, specifically relatable to context. The relationship between analysand and analyst is cited for two functions. The analyst being experienced as trustworthy, caring, reliable, and competent while involving the analysand in a method that promises and achieves help and benefit is a necessary foundation for the exploration to be possible. The relationship is commonly regarded as being an integral component of the treatment. For the analysand, treatment requires having a lengthy exposure to another human who is not only caring, trustworthy, and capable, but who permits his own narrative to enter the inquiry, to be challenged, criticized, subject to seductive attempts, and idealized. In addition, discovering the "who are you?" and "what do you mean to me?" that goes both ways contributes to the pervasive atmosphere. This transference–countertransference component of analysis not only makes the treatment possible, it is integral to the process itself.

We want to cite another aspect of the relationship: the ambiance that develops between analyst and analysand concurrent with the exploration, insight, and more adaptive seeking. While interpretation and interactive participation utilize verbal and nonverbal narratives involving discrete affects, intentions, and goals, the development and changes in ambiance involve a generalized affect tone – more atmospheric and holistic. *We* believe that, through an interrelated time line, *positive changes in the analysand–analyst ambiance facilitate positive modifications of the underlying affect tone.*

Clinical example: Mr. R, during a long period in his analysis, talked at great length about his fights and disagreements with his wife. They each had a remarkable facility to provoke the other. This pattern reflected the negativity in the family of each. Mr. R responded to his analyst pointing out his provocations in the sessions by exaggerated mea culpas – "Oh I am such a bad person" – this modeled after his mother who would feign suicide. The fighting between Mr. R and his wife was intensified on weekends, when neither worked and he had his analytic sessions. In a week when Mr. R described a number of incidents in which his wife was kind and sensitive, he reported they had gotten along well over the weekend. He welcomed the analyst's comment of "good" with the comment

> It was as though you were with me saying I really could choose – I didn't have to react to what I heard as a provocation – she may not have meant it that way. I think that is what you have been trying to get me to consider.

What was the process that led to Mr. R's different response to his wife over the weekend? Mr. R had long been aware of the pattern of his response to provocation, of his expectation and anticipation of it, and of his early life experience with his parents. We postulate that a change had occurred in the underlying affect tone, allowing a greater awareness of and response to affection both from his wife and his analyst. This change in underlying affect tone in turn potentiated the "good" weekend and was reflected in the changed ambiance between him and the analyst. This created a change in Mr. R's ability over the weekend to be an effective doer doing: initiating and responding, activating and taking in, resulting in further positive change in the underlying affect tone.

To go further, we encounter a difficulty: we must use words with the implication of narratives to describe what we mean by an underlying affect tone and its link to the extended timeline of analyst–analysand "working through" relational trends. Our assumption is that the underlying affect tone reflects sensitivities and sensibilities formed as emotional reflections of the maturing experiences of the three pathways for development. We identify a generalized feeling state that emerges from the success or failure to seek for an affectionate exchange, personal power and having one's skills appreciated, and bodily well-being and attractiveness. As the exploration in a successful analysis moves in the direction of successful seeking for affection, power, and bodily well-being, the changes will pass top-down to the underlying affect tone. This top-down passing of a positive development contributes to a lasting effect. The positive changes in the underlying tone will be reflected in largely nonsymbolic behaviors and attitudes: in more radiant smiles and greetings; in desires to hug and warmer handshakes; in posture and pace of stride; in the sureness of functional bodily movements; in attitudes of optimism, trust, and goodwill; in more musical and forceful or softened tonal quality in speech; in the range of gentleness and determination appropriate to the context. In all these ways, a person is himself affected and affects others

In our attempt to describe a negative affect tone becoming modified as a result of positive changes in the ongoing analyst–analysand ambiance, we are moving from discrete affects and symbolic processes to more generalized sensibilities. Our suggestion of "something more than" follows the formulations of both Daniel Stern (1971) and Jaak Panksepp (1998) whose versions differ but augment each other. Stern believed that by giving verbal representation to an experience, a person (especially an infant) moves away from its full intensity of impact. What contributes to the fullness of an affect experience is the vitality being felt: a something more than both the analytic relational ambiance and the underlying affect that we describe as more of a tone, a hum – a texture, a flavor, of the experience. The particular flavor or texture derives from the developments in each of the three pathways: sensibility reflecting affection and relatedness, and/or competence and power, and/or bodily well-being and regulation. All of the motivational systems play a part, but we believe the sensual system in its most elemental capacity to create both pleasurable enhancing arousal or desired calming and soothing is the primary contributor to a positive affect tone. Sensuality at its base has an auditory – musical – and visual – the smile – quality that emerges as sensorimotor activities flow in development and analysis. Panksepp, drawing primarily on brain studies, refers to "primary-process emotions" as "primal affects deeply subcortical" from which seeking emerges (Wright and Panksepp, 2012, p. 60).

> the prelinguistic nonpropositional understanding of the dynamic flow of movements valence defined as vitality affects or forms of vitality provides us with an appraisal of the interpersonal relations between the agent of the action and its recipient. This understanding goes beyond the action goal of what was done as it includes how it was performed (vigorously, haltingly, etc.).

Stern relates his findings to an infant's developing a capacity for relational knowing, and the discovery of motor neurons that helps to explain the ability of one person to infer the intentions inherent in another's actions. We believe the core sense of self (and the underlying affect component of it) is of a doer doing – activating and responding, imitating and taking in. As individuals we act with or on another – a person, an inanimate object, our body experienced as other (I bit my tongue). Or we are acted with or on by another – a person, an inanimate object (the ground just slipped from under me), or our body experienced it as other (my stomach is giving me a lot of trouble).

Conceptualizing the core sense of self or a doer doing as both intersubjective and interactive doer doing points toward a recognition that the experiences of self invariably includes a sense of "other" – subject and animate or inanimate object. The motivation inherent in each intention and goal can be regarded as seeking other – mother to hug, my rattle to play with, my finger to suck, my blanket and the reverie I create when alone in the presence of the other expresses the experience of presence during absence. Wanting to have time alone for work or reflection means including another as someone one wants to be free of.

When we reference "primary-process emotions" as "primary affects deeply subcortical" (Wright and Panksepp, 2012), or nonpropositional understanding of the dynamic flow of movements (Gallese and Goldman, 1998) or vitality forms of affect (Stern), or implicit relational knowing (BCDG, Boston Child Study Group), we are describing aspects of the ambiance that develops between analysand and analyst. And we are describing the underlying affect tone of the analysand as she experiences the ambiance. As the analysand exposes her inner state to gain insights and meaning, she becomes accessible to changes in her underlying affect tone – a process that occurs over extended time. The changes generally emerge out of awareness. The gains the changes reflect are perceptible only as changes in disposition, and as more animated and broadened seeking.

Shame, ideals, and identity

The Effect of Scolding and Shaming on the Intensity and Direction of Seeking: The Negative Effect on Identity of Personalizing Shame and Humiliation

In early infancy, fear and fright (Main, 1995), a chase and dodge failure in coordinating face-to-face communication (Beebe, et al., 2010), still-faced unresponsiveness (Tronick, et al., 1978), and maternal depression are all implicated in insecure attachment and a negative hedonic tone. In his seminal paper on affects, Tomkins (1981) stated that shame functions to inhibit mounting interest, pleasure, excitement, and enthusiasm. Along with its inhibiting effect, shame and scolding directly impact identity – the growing infant's sense of who he or she is. Timmy is delighted when his daddy picks him up. As Daddy is engaged in talking to Mother, Timmy's attention turns to Daddy's glasses, which take on the quality of an irresistibly alluring toy. As Timmy pulls on the glasses, Daddy states an emphatic "No! Naughty!" and pulls Timmy's hand away. Timmy hides his face in Daddy's neck, his body drooping.

Mother having left the room for a few minutes, Betty, no longer very hungry, starts to play with her food, mushing it about on her plate and the table. Seeing her little brother enter, she throws a piece at him. On her re-entry, Mother is startled and then, with an angry scold, finger wagging, tells a shame-faced Betty what a bad, bad girl she has been.

Billy starts a playful game of turning his head away as Mother tries to give him his bottle. Mother goes along with the game for a few minutes, then tells Billy to stop it, holds his head and Billy accepts the teat with a downward gaze.

Mother unexpectedly enters Mary's room to find Mary cooing in her bed as she leisurely rubs her genitals. Seeing mother, she jerks her hand from under the covers as mother gives her a look of embarrassed "oooh."

What do the parents of Timmy, Betty, Billy, and Mary hope will result from their interventions and their intensity? They hope that now or in response to repeated comparable interventions, their child will develop a signal of shame that has for him or her sufficient amplitude to curtail the amplitude of interest (the glasses), or messing (the food), or the pleasure of opposition (turning the head away), or the excitement of sexual arousal (masturbating). Having the capacity to signal to oneself implicitly or explicitly that "you will be ashamed if you act on that desire" is critical to regulate behavior that would be disadvantageous to the person's adaptation to live comfortably within his or her skin, family, group, or culture. A child's listening to his signaling to himself to stop a forbidden or destructive intention triggers an identity narrative: my mother thinks I am a good boy, and I feel it too.

Contemporary research indicates that infants repeatedly scolded and shamed for a particular behavior will anticipate and be hyper-responsive to the negative response of their caretakers. In some instances, a look saying "don't" from a mother is enough to lead the infant to inhibit the intention and have a shame affect and body-state change. The mother may provide an alternative route for the intention to play out – an optimal response. Or she may reward the infant's inhibition, saying with it "good boy." Or the infant, after the scold, will wait for the mother's attention to be diverted and resume his intention – shame transformed into the pleasure of defiance and being sneaky.

Donald Nathanson (1987) called shame "the underside of narcissism." What does this mean? In the Freudian tradition narcissism referred to regressive pathological grandiose preoccupation with self. The underside would be shame-filled preoccupation with self. In contrast, Morrison was writing from the perspective of Kohut. In self psychology, narcissism refers to healthy experiences of self-esteem, self-worth, and self-enhancement arising from being affirmed and having a kinship with and connection to admired others. If a person values herself as worthy and experiences her doings with pride, her underlying affect tone will have a generalized hum of heads-up optimism. If a person judges himself as deserving blame and rejection and experiences his doings with shame, his underlying affect tone will have a generalized hum of head-down pessimism.

How we currently construe the affects activated in Oedipal conflicts involves another shift in analytic theory bearing on shame. Freud's emphasis was largely on guilt and punishment, with very little mention of shame.

Guilt, we would agree, would be triggered by the Oedipal child's wish to do away with his or her rival parent. To harm or want to harm someone, especially a cared-about or loved parent, would arouse guilt. But other wishes in the Oedipal myth trigger different affects. The little boy comparing his penis with his adult father's may feel hopeful, excited, and enthusiastic about the future, or inferior, envious, and humiliated. The little girl comparing her genitals with a penis may feel defiantly equal or superior, or she may feel inferior, envious, and humiliated. Comparing her flat chest with her mother's breasts, she may feel hopeful about the future, or inferior and envious. Both boy and girl wanting what he and she know is forbidden in their family and their culture – sexing with a parent, each other, a boy with a boy, a girl with a girl, and masturbating – will feel mixtures of excitement and shame. In each of these contexts, whether guilt, humiliation, or shame, the result can be a defiant denial of the restrictions of the prohibition. Alternatively, with an underlying affect tone of power common to sociopathic individuals, bouts of shame and inhibition of the urge may trigger resignation, loss, and sadness with an underlying affect tone of lowered vitality and optimism.

Sensuality and sexuality across the divide of shame

Sammy, at 3 months, and his mother have established a comfortable feeding rhythm. As he sucks, his little fist against her breast slowly opens and his small fingers stroke her soft skin. Experiencing the pleasurable tactile sensations, she looks down lovingly at him as they jointly enjoy the sensuality. She thinks "Sammy is a loving boy. He loves me."

Now, move ahead to Sammy at 3 ½ years old. Seeing his sad and angry look, his mother allows him to climb up next to her as she breastfeeds his baby sister. Calming from his initial fussing at exclusion, Sammy begins to look with fascination at the sucking baby and his mother's breast. Sammy starts to reach for her breast, and his mother rebukes him: "No. No. Sammy you mustn't." She thinks Sammy has become a naughty boy. His interest/excitement inhibited, Sammy looks downcast and crushed before he begins to protest again.

In both of the observations, Sammy is drawn to the sensual pleasure of touching his mother's breast. In the first instance, his touch is welcomed by a mirroring glance from his mother, who is pleased and happy to share their rising pleasurable exchange. I suggest it is as if she were saying to him: "Sammy you are a sensual little boy, and I am a sensual woman, and together we can enjoy sensuality without shame or maybe with just the tiniest hint of embarrassment on my part." In the second observation, a similar interest in pleasure is no longer responded to with pleasurable acceptance and sharing. As with most experiences, the motives are complex. Sammy's initial fuss is anger and envy at his mother shutting out and replacing him with his sister, and his mother tries to respond by offering him inclusion. The central component of the experience is Sammy's hand reaching to touch his mother's breast. The motivation behind his gesture includes wanting to have what his sister has, but mainly, I believe, he is reactivating a somatic memory and an underlying affect tone of a pleasurable sensual experience generalized from repeated experiences before his weaning.

So, what has changed? Probably outside of her awareness, Sammy's mother is influenced by two different value systems prescribed by her culture. One evaluation concludes the young baby's touching, exploring, and fondling are innocent of intentions regarded as naughty, dirty, or even perverse. Innocent intentions to arouse pleasurable body–mind experiences – intentions I refer to as *sensual* – are not regarded by Sammy's mother as threats to excite her or Sammy. She does not attribute to herself or Sammy an intrusion of lustful desire into their personal Garden of Eden.

Sammy's mother uses a different value system to evaluate the actions and intentions of the 3 1/2-year-old, who she sees as wanting to play with her breast, demarcated at this point as a sexual body part. Collateral annoyance at Sammy for interfering with the ongoing feeding may have accentuated her irritability but is not central to her message: "You may not fondle my breast." More precisely, the message was:

> Curb your excitement, curb that kind of action and the arousal it aims for and will generate. Your intention, if not impeded, will lead to actions and excitement that are shameful. You, and we, will have crossed the line that divides what is "innocent," acceptable, containable, affectionate *sensuality* from what is unacceptable, dangerously arousing, lustful, *sexuality*.

Once shamed, Sammy casts his eyes down, his posture slumps, and his lips turn down at the sides. He does not remain long in the shame state but moves into an irritable sulk. Climbing off the chair that holds his mother and sister, he begins to throw his toys. This brings on another, now angry, admonition from mother for him to stop. "Bad boy" now combines sexual badness (actually a gentle movement of his arm to fondle the breast) with angry destructive badness (the more violent movement of his arms throwing his toys). In Sammy's lived experience, the relatively straightforward, "innocent," sensually motivated gesture is converted, first, into a mildly conflictual "naughty" sexual desire through mother's shaming restraint; and, second, through the subsequent temper protest and mother's intensified shaming prohibition, into a conflict over willfulness. Sammy is at risk for forming an identity as a sulky, willful child with an underlying affect tone of irritability and grumpiness.

To summarize, sensuality involves a pleasurable body sensation that can be shared with another who looks on (mirrors) the activity benignly as participant or witness. Sensuality may also involve a pleasurable body sensation when alone, accompanied by an afterimage or fantasy of a mirroring other implicitly conveying approval. Sensuality originates in infancy as body-generated experiences that can be elaborated in imagination, fantasies, and dream imagery into mini-narratives. Throughout life, imagination, fantasy, and dream imagery can activate or intensify body-generated sensual experiences associated with an underlying affect tone of a pleasant glow.

Sexuality involves a pleasurable body sensation that, when sought by a child, often is interrupted by a prohibiting response. For a developing child or adolescent, sexuality is a "package" that combines a desire based on memory of a prior pleasurable sensation or an immediate body sensation urge (itch) and an authority who, rather than mirror, share, and comfortably regulate the flow of the urge, prohibits its fulfillment. The child or adolescent may see him or herself as a sensual/sexual who follows the rules and stays out of trouble, or flirts with the edges, testing how much he or she can get away with before shame hits, or who adds episodes of defiant rebellion – enjoying not only the exciting sexual doing but the powerful feeling of being unrestrained.

The reverberating circuit of shame

Professor Black, a committed member of Procrastinators Anonymous, followed a regular pattern of accomplishment. She would start her day painfully, shamefully remembering she hadn't performed a task she had promised herself, her students, or her school she would do. She would be setting out to do it when it would occur to her to check her email for anything new. Then it would occur to her that she had a call to make, or a note to write, or a text to answer, and she would get all involved in that. Then, with a great pinch of shame, she would remember the put-off task. The shame feeling was such an unpleasant intrusion into her busy doing state that she would want to put it out of her mind as soon as possible. A bite to eat or a chat with a friend or call to Procrastinators Anonymous would help to eradicate the immediacy of the unwelcome emergence of shame. The shame-reducing diversion of course added to her feeling of irresponsibility and presented a further source of shame. She might then gear up to tackle the avoided task. For a brief time feel she would feel relieved, with a moment of pride, until she remembered the next task she had been putting off and the shame would return. Both her parents had been critical and perfectionistic but offered little help to her in achieving her intentions and goals. Her underlying affect tone reflected feelings of being alone, with a mix of high energy and being helpless to focus without a guiding hand.

Shame as identity

Johnny *you did a really bad thing* crayoning on our newly painted wall. We'll get something to clean it off.

Tom *you are a really bad boy*. You never listen. You just want to drive me crazy. Go to your room. I don't want to see you – you upset me so much!

Johnny is told he *acted* in an unacceptable way. He should be ashamed of his *behavior*. He must learn to change what he *does*.

Tom is told he *should be ashamed of his very being*: he is a bad doer, an obstinate refuser to learn, a threat to his mother's sanity, and his whole physical being is a disturbing sight to see.

Johnny is given the space to use shame as a signal to inhibit an inclination to mar a surface not designated for crayoning. Johnny's mother said *we* will work it out, introducing a "we" – a "you and I," a spirit of cooperation. She might add "Next time I'll see you have a nice book to crayon in."

Tom is given no space to develop reflection about a specific intention. He isn't only acting badly, *he* is bad – the whole of his being. Mother says the problem is him: his shameful badness. For her, it's all bad-boy Tom's fault. She polarizes. Where Johnny's mother might have an implicit experience of signal shame that she wasn't there to supervise Johnny, Tom's mother has no such self-reflective experience. And Tom gets no space for his own self-reflection. He too will polarize. He may accept her designation, build it into his identity, into his sense of self, and accommodate to it. Or he may internally roil against her attribution and conclude implicitly or explicitly that *she* is a bad, mean mommy. Tom's internal message to himself – often deeply felt – is that his naughtiness aside, he is not bad or evil and that his accuser is treating him in a manner that demonstrates no loving care and fairness. Tom is far more likely to make this more positive if he has built a reservoir of loving, caring belief in his essential goodness from the treatment of significant others who like him and react to his unacceptable acts as Johnny's mother did.

Respect for a child's intentions and a balance between praise and shame-scolding increases the likelihood for reflective space and signaling to inhibit unacceptable intentions. Repetitive scolding, especially if accompanied by threats and fear, diminishes the likelihood of reflective space. Scolding and threats expressed in tones of disdain, condescension, and contempt have a lasting corrosive effect on self-respect, as do with shame and humiliation. The corrosive effect will include an underlying affect tone of being unlovable, and of lacking self-confidence or hope in seeking.

Clinical example

Mr. T's mother often responded to anything her child did that upset her – commonly ordinary activities – with hysterical intensity. She would scold, threaten to abandon the family, or make suicidal gestures. Mr. T's father was often unavailable or might respond to an upset in the home with an angry outburst. Both parents considered Mr. T to be a bad boy, and Mr. T accepted this attribution. He developed a speech defect based on fear and would place himself at risk in the rough neighborhood in which he lived. He also developed a pattern of defiantly enacting unacceptable mean, exhibitionistic, and sometimes antisocial behaviors that continued into adulthood. Alongside his fear of attack and rejection, his risk taking, and his antisocial acts, he developed adaptive behaviors that, combined with his high intelligence, propelled him into a successful career. In his analysis he often would bring up a current insensitive or antisocial behavior or the memory of one of the many examples from the past. These revelations triggered a momentary experience of shame or guilt that rapidly was lost as a guiding signal. Rather than stay with the shame or guilt, his tone would shift to one of pleasurable defiance followed by exaggerated statements of what an awful person he was. His defiant exaggerations of his badness were dramatizations of a shame state that seemed to both of us a mimicry and mockery of his mother's histrionics. In this state, his message to me, and to the world, was

> OK if you are going to give me a hard time and scold and blame me, I'll show you what bad really is – I'll smash this phone or block your path with my car and you can hit me and damage your car.

At these moments he was in a state completely dissociated from his highly skilled cooperative professional persona. By retaining his bad-boy identity he was able to turn shame into the pride and sadistic pleasure he derived from defiance of rules, restraints, and authorities.

Mr. W's mother had been unprotected and traumatically abused as a young woman, a fact that became known to Mr. W only as an adult. As a child, what Mr. W experienced was his mother's excessive reaction to his little-boy teasing of his younger sister. Caught in their mother's distorted projection of her traumatic abuse onto her daughter as victim and her son as destructive abuser, the two children played out their roles in a continuous drama. The little girl would scream "Mother, he's looking at me! Mother, he's pointing his finger at me!" The mother would come rushing in to comfort her upset daughter and scold and shame her bad, bad, bad little boy. Seduced by her role of protected victim, the little girl did all she could to provoke his responses. Later, at school age, Mr. W, enacting his bad-boy role, became the class clown. This led to him frequently being sent being to the principal's office, a happening his sister eagerly announced to her parents. Mr. W's father remained a passive observer, reluctant to cross his wife and trigger her anger. Mr. W remembers his father on one occasion saying "You're a cry baby" to his daughter and "You're a tease" to his son. His father contributed one component to Mr. W's bad-boy identity by his demand for perfectionism in any task he assigned to his son.

At the same time as Mr. W saw himself as bad, he also recognized he was a person of considerable charm, friendliness, capability, caring, and sensitivity to others. His prevailing sense of self was characterized by a constant feeling that he disappointed others, seeing everywhere he looked an indication of his shameful neglect. In his more fleeting sense of self he recognized his many accomplishments and his great professional success. This confusing dichotomy of identity has its origin in the dichotomy of his mother's responses to him. In his initial 18 months of life, before the birth of his sister, his mother had been loving and devoted. The difficulty began with the birth of a daughter with whom she had identified as desperately needing protection from a male predator – not her passive, avoidant husband, but the lively vibrant little boy. This whole context was compartmentalized to the triad of protective mother, victim daughter, and predator son. But outside of that context, Mr. W's mother was attentive, caring, and proud of her achieving son. These two dissociated states continued throughout Mr. W's adult years, when his mother would suddenly turn on him with shaming scolds when he said something to his sister's children that would be innocuous to anyone else. This would also provoke his sister into an episode of highly dramatized victimization.

The recurrence and persistence of his "being bad" identity in the minds of mother and sister and his acting it out as class clown led to Mr. W's skewed view of himself in the world. Fiercely ambitious, he demanded advancement and fairness from others. Simultaneously, he was continually scolding and shaming himself for tasks set aside or not completed. As it impacted his mood, reflecting his underlying affect tone of helplessness to alter his negative identity, he had a very low threshold for seeing failings and experiencing shame, and a high threshold for seeing himself as worthy despite generally receiving high praise from others. He consistently scanned his internal and external world for evidence of what he should have done but did not do. The persistent shame that resulted from his scanning led to his resignation that nothing would or could change for the better. Mr. W's chronic shame state and his resignation to it led to an abiding underlying affect tinge of sadness. He experienced brief moments of joy from the accolades he received from important people that he impressed, and longer moments of pleasure when he could be by himself, free of obligation. Despite living many aspects of a successful life, admired by many others and offering wise advice and caring to friends and family members, he was endlessly stalked by an embodied sense of shame. Trapped in never knowing whether to believe the accusation originating from his delusional mother's trauma that he was dangerous made him unable to have good experiences, which had an impact on his underlying affect tone of helpless pessimism.

Goodwill

Goodwill is not a term commonly used in psychoanalytic discourse. Goodwill has the opposite effect of shame. While shame limits the recognition of positive intent and experience and curbs inquiry, goodwill is open to the positive and to further exploration. Clinically, the absence of goodwill on the part of a patient toward those with whom he associates is a serious failing. Failure to approach others with goodwill leads a reduction of positive experiences, invites others to be wary and oppositional, and results in a deprivation of the sense of self. A major source for the development of goodwill in a person's approach to his endeavors with others emerges from experiences central to the attachment, affiliative, sensual-sexual, and exploratory motivational systems. Do the parents contain and work out their inevitable frustrations with the child, other children, and with each other? Or is family life characterized by arguments, disrespect, scolding, shaming, and disdain? Do the parents listen with open minds and give each other and their children the benefit of the doubt, or do they jump immediately to assumptions of negative intent?

In analysis, an analyst's goodwill is more than her technical skill, dedication, emphatic listening, and openness to relate. What more? The analyst seeks and responds to aspects of the analysand's intentions that can be respected and affirmed. This openness of an analyst to welcome what she can affirm and support must be present when the analyst decides to accept the person as an analysand. Then, expectations based on goodwill can expand as more and more aspects of the analysand's improvements are recognized. The explicit recognition of adaptive changes brought about by the treatment are reflected by implicit changes in the ambiance between analyst and analysand. Implicitly, the analysand can feel she wants the analyst to see, recognize, and help her with her problems. But even when immersed in conflicts and maladaptive choices, the analysand implicitly wants the assurance of the analyst's goodwill – the readiness to see him as a worthy, caring human being, a person who exhibits positive intentions and goals even when conflicted and antagonistic. Does an expanding optimistic underlying affect tone lead the patient to expect that her intentions are likely to be accepted by others? Or that the problems that emerge will be approached with efforts to come to an acceptable solution?

In the beginning of his analysis, Mr. G began many of his sessions by saying things such as "You're not going to like what I did"; "You'll think I shouldn't have sent the email to my daughter about her spending." If I picked up on his uncertainty about an action he had taken, he would begin to berate himself in a fashion that mirrored the exaggerated, hysterical tone of his mother or the finger-wagging put-downs of his father. Although very knowledgeable, he was reluctant to attend social gatherings because he would assume that he had nothing to say that would interest someone until he was greeted with a reassuring, warm welcome. He would find a negative in any of my interventions – wasting his time, his money, failing to see what he had done wrong. He saw his sadness as just a plea for pity that he did not deserve. Stated differently, he had no goodwill for himself, or for my efforts to help him, and for a long time he did not experience goodwill from me. All he could hope for was pity. As we worked with the negative assumptions, Mr. G began to establish a small number of relationships in which the positive regard for his intentions – a manifestation of goodwill – could come to the fore. This shifting pattern was reflected in the ambiance between us, and Mr. G began to openly value the sessions and miss them during absences. A shift in underlying affect tone was reflected in a lessening of desperation and his prior addictive use of alcohol. More situations in his life were approached with an implicit assumption that goodwill would be present.

Cultural values and idealized narratives

Heroics: a masculine ideal

From the playground to the battleground, a boy's/man's assertiveness, aggressiveness, daring, and courage build pride. Alternatively, being a sissy, a nerd, a patsy, or a pansy brings shame, humiliation, and disdain.

David's mother discovered welts all over her 13-year-old son's back. Getting no explanation from David, she consulted other mothers. She discovered that a cult had formed, led by a classmate of David's. The boys would meet in the exercise room where the leader, Luke, would point to a boy to be struck with a whip. Luke being the son of a rich donor led the faculty to turn a blind eye. The unprotected boys made it a virtue to never tell. To take the whipping was to be manly; to tell was to be a wimp and squealer, a tattle-tale – a shameful act.

In her evocative paper "The Myth of the Hero," Chana Ullman (2016) describes the frequent, extreme shame that emerged in the analysis of many soldiers with PTSD. The repeated pattern was that the soldier was tortured by shame, humiliation, and guilt associated with a failure to live up to his ideal of courage. The analyst herself felt torn with counter feelings of admiration for their bravery and service. She knew that if she verbalized her perspective it would sadly have come across as unempathetic to the deep feelings of the soldier about a buddy he should have rescued or an attack on the enemy he had taken too long to launch.

On a less dramatic scale is the shame of the bystander who didn't intervene when his close friend was being beaten up by a bully. Or the boxer who could have gotten up and fought more when knocked down but didn't. These specific events in the life of a boy or man will reappear in dreams or associations stirred by their frequent dramatization in movies – like who did or did not make a heroic sacrifice on the Titanic.

When we move from a structural hypothesis to an experience-based approach, values and ideals are integrated with what is being sought, what is being intended, what goals guide the doer's doings. In fantasies and dreams, values and ideals are holistically included. And the underlying affect tone that reflects the doer doing's holistic inclusion of whether ideals being met must lead to a feeling of being good or not being met lead to a feeling of failing.

Superwoman: a feminine ideal

Superwoman can do it all. She can have a successful career. She can be a sexual partner and intimate companion of her husband's. She can be a sensitive, available, and caring mother. And she can have a group of close, "best" female friends. Of course, many – maybe most – women would not subscribe to this remarkable ideal in its fullest. For those who do, failure to achieve this entire ideal way of being would trigger disappointment, shame, and humiliation. Or others, who maintain the ideal but have to abandon one or another of its components, would feel like a humiliating sacrifice had to be made. When she would see or imagine a woman who she believed "had it all," she would feel the shame of inferiority. Especially painful for many women is failure in mothering. Women who are unable to have children – either to become pregnant or to carry a pregnancy full term – often experience feelings of disappointment and shame and a deep sense of their body letting them down. Whether pulled by career or a demanding husband, a mother of children whom she finds she cannot fully love and/or know how to care for will oscillate between shame, guilt, and resentment, with depression as a frequent outcome. Another pitfall of the goal of doing it all, even only some of it all, is the strain it puts on marriage. Often couples whose sexual rhythms and appetites coincided richly during courting or early marriage later find it difficult to get in sync with each other's desires. Shame may be triggered for refusing and/or for being refused – shame and humiliation at feeling not sexy enough or not attractive enough for the other is a depressing inhibiter of sensual pleasure and orgiastic excitement. Boys and girls, men and women rely on same gender friends for a particularly satisfying type of intimacy – whether sport teams, social clubs, or weekly lunches or drinks together. However, we believe that for girls, especially beginning in early adolescence, "best friends" are particularly significant for a sense of deep comradery. A woman's desire for this deep intimacy can, and often does, continue throughout life. Women who don't have women friends, who can't form, or who can't maintain those friendships are apt to wonder shamefully what is wrong with them, sometimes jokingly saying "do I have BO?" – a clear reference to the embarrassment of rejection.

We need to add several caveats to what we state here about male and female ideals. Women in combat, as soldiers and nurses, may experience PTSD and similar conflicts and shame as men. Some men also may have issues of "wanting it all" similar to what we describe for women. Comparable to boys not wanting to be shamed as a tattle-tale, woman regard leaking a friend's confidence as a source of shame and guilt. An important caveat is that I have essentially used descriptions and examples that apply to heterosexual relations. If we examined the experiences of homosexual and transgender men and women, we would find both similar and different avenues for the triggering of shame, embarrassment, humiliation, shyness, disappointment, and guilt, with homophobia as an additional source of shame.

In many instances of pathological shame, the groupings of past and present pride memories will be few. In other instances, like for Mr. T and Mr. W, the past and present pride memories are frequently dissociated. Because of the dissociation, an experience of being successful in carrying out an intention has little or no effect on the amount of or receptivity of shame. In therapy, the analyst needs to recognize and emphasize any experience in which a goal that would have led to shame is implicitly or explicitly dealt with adaptively – like, say, an adolescent turning off the computer game and doing his homework. As we explore a patient's shame sequence, we can bring into focus the feelings and details of that experience. To do so is itself shaming. So sharing with empathy and compassion what has been brought into focus is a step forward. Then what? Does the patient *alter* the shame-activating pattern (begin to come on time)? Or does the patient continue the pattern, thereby adding to the shame? In treatment, both repeating the shame pattern and acting to reverse it will occur. But with what frequency does acting to reverse the pattern occur, and what may be the determining factor? Let's return to Johnny's, mother who stayed with him after the shaming episode and said "We will get something to clean it off." We believe a parent responding like that provides a selfobject experience that serves as an internalized model of constructive repair of both the damage to the wall and to the relationship. As shame appears in the treatment, either as reactivated in memory recall or as enacted in the present, does the patient experience the therapist as Tom's mother seeing him as bad, or as Johnny's mother staying with him during and outside the session to help him make a repair? If like Johnny's mother helping him make the repair, the underlying affect tone of being a bad, unlovable child will diminish and the possibility of seeing himself as worthy of praise and love will rise – probably ever-so – gradually.

Ever-so gradually? Why does it take so long? Why is pathological shame so difficult to treat? With other dystonic affective experiences, such as sadness or pain, we are naturally motivated to be free of the negative state. But the state of being ashamed and whatever was responsible for activating that feeling tend to make the patient feel more ashamed as the issue surfaces in the course of the treatment. Openness to regard the new experiences as shameful is strong and the expectation is high. This reverberation of conscious and underlying shame results in a motive to hide and avoid rather than to access the feeling and context. And repetitive shame is more than a feeling we experience in the cognitive realm; pathological shame is experienced deep in the body, affecting facial expression, with head and eyes downcast, droopy body posture, and slower pace and movements. Equally insidious is the penetration into the generalized holistic sense of self, of identity, of low self-worth, of badness. Additionally, living with chronic shame has a secondary effect of souring the individual's disposition, often leading to a depressive irritable, emotional cast and a resigned, cynical approach – a state of mind that says "What is the use of being around people? They won't want to see me the way I am, and I don't want to see them and feel rejected and more ashamed." This negative drag, both physical and emotional, may coexist with an entirely different split-off adaptive productive mode of being and functioning. However, the negative, downward feeling state is most often triggered in relationships – especially intimate relationships. Consequently, in the exploratory treatment of patients with chronic shame, the emergence of the patient's shame emotions combined with his or her reluctance to expose the feelings and the triggering events in and out of the treatment will test the therapist's patience and resourcefulness. A therapist's positive hopefulness will at times be helpful in carrying the treatment forward. At other times, positive hopefulness will come across as denial and a failure to appreciate empathetically not only the patient's conscious and underlying feeling of being stuck, but also the influence on the dyad of the depressive irritable emotional ambiance. "Being with" when a downward cast intensifies is difficult for both patient and therapist, but is crucial for the work of intersubjective understanding and establishing a benign intrapsychic presence that leads to the patient's emergence from repetitive shame state experiences and alteration of an underlying affect tone of feeling bad, unloving, and being unlovable – with little hope for change.

Summary

In Chapter 1, we have presented concepts that derive from a focus on experience in research, observation, analytic treatment, and theory: seeking, three pathways for development, an underlying affect tone, the role of a developing ambiance between analyst and analysand, and the effect of shaming on identity. We believe that an integration and synthesis of these concepts offers an enlivened narrative of many aspects of human motivation, development, and implicit and explicit human experience.

References

Alcaro, A. and Panksepp, J. (2011). The SEEKING Mind: primal neuro-affective substrates for appetitive incentive states and their pathological dynamics in addictions and depression. *Neuroscience Biobehavioral Reviews*, 35 (9): 1805–1820.

Beebe, B., Jaffe, J., Markese, S., Buck, K., Chen, H., Cohen, P.... Feldstein, S. (2010). The origins of 12-month attachment: a microanalysis of 4-month mother-infant interaction. *Attachment and Human Development*, 12: 3–141.

Beebe, B. and Lachmann, F. (2002). *Infant research and adult treatment: Co-constructing interactions*. Hillsdale, NJ: The Analytic Press.

Bower, T. (1971). The object in the world of the infant. *Scientific American.*, 225: 30–38.

Bowlby, J. (1973). Attachment and loss. Vol. 2 *Separation*. New York: Basic Books.

Bowlby, J. (1988). *A secure base: Clinical applications of attachment theory*. London: Routledge.

Brazelton, T.B. (1980). New knowledge about the infant from current research: Implications for psychoanalysis. Presented to the American Psychoanalytic Association, San Francisco, May 3.

Brazelton, T.B. and Als, H. (1979). Four early stages in the development of mother-infant-interaction. *The Psychoanalytic Study of the Child*, 34: 349–371.

Bruner, J. and Sherwood, V. (1980). Thought, language, and interaction in infancy. Presented to the First World Congress on Infant Psychiatry, Portugal, March 30–April 3.

Bucci, W. (1957). *Psychoanalysis and cognitive science: A multiple code theory*. New York, NY: Guilford Press.

Call. J. (1980). Some prelinguistic aspects of language development. *Journal of American Psychoanalytic Association*, 28: 259–290

Carpenter, G. (1974). Mother's face and the newborn. *New Scientist*, 61: 742.

Condon, W., and Sander, L. (1972). Neonate movement is synchronized with adult speech. *Science*, 183: 99–101.

DeCasper, A.J. and Fifer, W.P. (1980). Of human bonding: newborns prefer their mother's voices. *Science.* New Series, 208 (4448): 1174–1176.

Eimas, P.D., Siqueland, E.R., Jusczyk, P., and Vigorito, J. (1971). Speech preparation in infants. *Science*, New Series, 171 (3968): 303–306.

Gallese, V. and Goldman, A. (1998). Mirror neurons and the simulation theory of mind-reading. Elsevier Science. *Trends in Cognitive Science*, 2(12): 493–501.

Hamlin, J.K., Wynn, K., and Bloom, P. (2007). Social evaluaton by preverbal infants. *Nature*, 450: 557–560

Hamlin, J.K., Wynn, K., and Bloom, P. (2010). Three-month-olds show a negativity bias in their social interactions. *Developmental Science*, 13 (6): 923–929.

Klin, A., Jones, W., Schultz, R., Volkman, F., and Cohen, D., (2003). Defining and qualifying the social phenotype in autism. Am. J. Psychiatry, 159 (6): 895–907.

Kohut, H. (1971). *An analysis of the self: A systematic approach to the psycho-analytic treatment of narcissistic personality disorder*. Chicago: University of Chicago Press.

Lichtenberg, J. (1973). Book review: *The analysis of self* by Heinz Kohut. Bulletin Philadelphia Association of Psychoanalysis, 23: 58–66.

Lichtenberg, J. (1981). The empathic mode of perception and alternative vantage points for psychoanalytic work. *Psychoanalytic Inquiry,* 1(3) 329–355.

Lichtenberg, J. (1989a). Psychoanalysis and Motivation. Hillsdale, NJ: The Analytic Press

Lichtenberg, J. (1989b). Psychoanalytic theory is a many splendored thing: A discussion of discussions. *Psychoanalytic Inquiry,* 9 (4): 586–603.

Lichtenberg, J. (1991). What is SelfObject? *Psychoanalytic Dialogues,* 1:455–479.

Lichtenberg, J. (2008). *Sensuality and sexuality across the divide of shame.* New York: The Analytic Press.

Lichtenberg, J., Lachmann, F., and Fossage, J. (1989). *Psychoanalysis and motivation.* Hillsdale, NJ: The Analytic Press.

Lichtenberg, J., Lachmann, F., and Fosshagem J. (1992). *Self and motivational systems.* Hillsdale, NJ: The Analytic Press.

Lichtenberg, J., Lachmann, F., and Fosshage, J. (1996). *The clinical exchange: Technique from the standpoint of self and motivational systems.* Hillsdale, NJ: The Analytic Press.

Lichtenberg, J., Lachmann, F., and Fosshage, J. (2011). *Psychoanalysis and motivational systems: A new look.* New York, NY: Routledge

Lichtenberg, J., Lachmann, F., and Fosshage, J. (2017). *Narrative and meaning: The foundation of mind, creativity and the psychoanalytic dialogue.* New York, NY: Routledge.

Lichtenberg, J. and Thielst, S. (2018). *From autism and mutism to an enlivened self - a case narrative with reflections on early development.* London: Routledge.

Main, M. (1995). Recent studies in attachment: Overview, with selected implications for clinical work. In S. Goldberg, R. Muir, and J. Kerr (Eds.), *Attachment Theory: Social, developmental and clinical perspectives*, pp. 407–470. Hillsdale, NJ: Analytic Press, Inc.

Morrison, A. (1989). *Shame: The underside of narcissism.* Hillsdale, NJ: The Analytic Press.

Moss, H. and Robson, K. (1968). The role of protest behavior in the development of mother-infant attachment. Presented to the American Psychological Association, San Francisco.

Nathanson, D. (Ed.) (1987). *The many faces of shame.* New York: Guilford Press.

Panksepp, J. (1998). *Affective neuroscience: The foundations of human and animal emotions*. Oxford University Press: New York.

Perani, D., Dehaene, S., Grassi, F., Cohen, L., Cappa, S., Dupoux, E., Fazio, F., and Mehler, J., (1996). Brain processing of native and foreign languages. *Cognitive Neuroscience and Neuropsychology*, Vol. 7, No. 15–17, November.

Roth, P. (2013). *Portnoy's complaint* [1969]. Penguin Random House, LLC.

Schore, A. (1994). *Affect regulation and the origin of the self*. Hillsdale, NJ: Erlbaum.

Schulz, R. PhD, Gauthier, I. PhD, Klin, A. PhD, Fulbright, R. MD, Anderson, A. PhD, Voklmar, F. MD, Skudlarski, P. PhD, Lacadie, C. BS, Cohen, D. MD, and Gore, J. PhD. (2000). Abnormal ventral temporal cortical activity during face discrimination among individuals with Autism and Asperger Syndrome. *Arch Gen Psychiatry*, 57: 331–340.

Spitz, R. A. (1957). *No and Yes: On the genesis of human communication*. Oxford, England: International Universities Press

Stern, D. (1971). A microanalysis of mother-infant interaction. *Journal of American Academy of Child and Adolescent Psychiatry*, 10: 501–517.

Stern, D. (1977). *The first relationship*. Cambridge, Mass: Harvard University Press.

Stern, D. (1985). *The interpersonal world of the infant: A view from psychoanalysis and development*. New York, NY: Basic Books.

Stern, D. (1990). *Diary of a baby: What your child sees, feels, and experiences*. New York, NY: Basic Books.

Stolorow, R., Brandschaft, B. and Atwood, G. (1983). Intersubjectivity in psychoanalytic treatment. *Bulletin of the Menninger Clinic*, (47) 2.

Terhune, C. (1979). The role of hearing in early ego organization. *The Psychoanalytic Study of the Child*, 34: 349–370. New Haven, CT: Yale University Press.

Tomkins, S. (1981). The quest for primary motives: Biography and autobiography of an idea: *Journal of Personality and Social Psychology*, 41:306–329.

Trevarthen, C. (1977). Descriptive analyses of infant communication behavior. In H. Schaffer (Ed.), *Studies in Mother–Infant Interaction*, pp. 227–270. London: Academic Press.

Tronick, E., Als, J., Adamson, L., Wise, S., & Brazelton, T. (1978). The infant's response to entrapment between contradictory messages in face-to-face interaction. *Journal of the American Academy of Child & Adolescent Psychiatry*, 17: 1–13.

Ullman, C. (2016). The Myth of the Hero. Paper presented at IARPP Conference. Rome, Italy.

Winnicott, D. (1941). The observation of infants in a set situation. *International Journal of Psychoanalysis.*, 22: 229–249.

Winnicott, D.W. (1953). Transitional objects and transitional phenomena – A study of the first not-me possession, *International Journal of Psychoanalysis.*, 34: 89–97.

Winnicott, D.W. (1956). *Primary maternal preoccupation through paediatrics to psychoanalysis.* London: Hogarth.

Winnicott, D.W. (1958). The capacity to be alone. *International Journal of Psychoanalysis.*, 39: 416–420.

Winnicott, D.W. (1965). The maturational processes and the facilitating environment: Studies in the theory of emotional development. *International Psycho-Analytic Library*, 64: 1–276. London: The Hogarth Press and the Institute of Psycho-Analysis.

Wright, J. and Panksepp J. (2012). An evolutionary framework to understand foraging, wanting, and desire: The neuropsychology of the SEEKING system. *Neuropsychoanalysis*, 14 (1).

Chapter 2

The treatment of Eileen

Introduction

We present the story of Eileen, whose trauma in early life left her with a deep, underlying affect tone of shame and anxiety about being found to be unattractive and of little worth despite having been a successful professional. We will illustrate the continuity of Eileen's negative identity despite prior attempts in therapy and positive alterations in her life accomplishments and styles in each of the three pathways: seeking prideful human relations, skills in learning and functioning as a physician, and being well-groomed and physically healthy. Eileen's underlying pervasive shame persisted despite her analyst's (FML) skillful standing in the space as a participant-observer affirming her current accomplishments in her professional pursuits and analytic linking of past and present.

We regard the basis of interrupting the continuity of Eileen's negative shame states as a result of an intersubjective deep appreciation from the analyst's own life experience of struggle with shame activated by Eileen's dream representation of him. Moments of emotional twinship triggered a different ambiance – a deeper sense of sharing the pain of disappointment crystallized around appearance. Eileen had hoped to overcome her shame by finding a taller and richer man – a solution at the practical symbolic level. Her analyst's emotional sharing introduced an ambiance between them that combined appreciation of her deep sense of shame – a pathologic identity – with an appreciation that the underlying sense of self-humiliation can give way to a hum of being worthy, bright, accomplished, affectionate, and sexual.

Continuity and change (FL)

Psychoanalytic theorists (for example, Jacobson, 1967) have emphasized the experience of self-sameness in spite of change in discussions of identity. But little has been proposed as to how that self-sameness is achieved, maintained, and repeated. Change is often conceptualized as change over time. In spite of growing older, we maintain a sense of identity, of who we feel ourselves to be, of self-sameness, in spite of the adjustments to the challenges of time. To explain how smoothly we are able to shift from one motivational system to another, we (Lichtenberg, Lachmann, and Fosshage, 2011) explicated the theory of fractals. We now apply this concept to the maintenance of self-sameness, the sense of self.

In Chapter 1, we identified three developmental paths that we now propose become significant in psychoanalytic treatment. These are the paths of development that lead to a capacity for intimacy in relationships, to mastery and competence in the world of work and play, and to attention to one's body appearance and physical well-being. We now apply these developmental concepts and fractal theory to psychoanalytic treatment, specifically as related to the organization and experience of the sense of self.

Fractals refer to repetitive patterns found in nature. Fractals can be illustrated in how a tree grows, how clouds form, the structure of a snowflake, or the shape of a coastline. In each case, one small piece – a fractal – has the major, defining characteristics of the whole. Of particular relevance for the sense of self is the simultaneous presence of firm boundaries in conjunction with open boundaries. This is most clearly illustrated in the shape of clouds and their simultaneous open boundaries when they converge with other clouds and become one newly shaped cloud.

Fractal theory is a specialized theory of nonlinear dynamic systems that we used in explicating motivational systems. The consistency of identity, of a core sense of self, despite the varied experiences of different stages of life shift our focus to processes that underlie experiences of adaptive alteration of patterns in successful analysis.

We argued that self-similarity of affects, intentions, and goals, and their frequent repetitions, identify the fractal nature of the seven motivational systems and of the system as a whole. We also recognized the open boundaries of fractals that enable clouds, as illustrated above, to combine with other clouds and yet retain a bounded shape. With respect to motivational systems, openness enables collusion among different motivational systems such as attachment, sexuality, and caretaking. Once we have postulated these smooth shifts, we are well on our way to recognizing similar smoothness in the shifting experience of our sense of self.

Maintaining self-sameness requires recognition and integration of how we regard ourselves to be, how other regard us to be, how we wish to be regarded, as well as how we dread to be regarded. In the present study of focusing on "seeking" and experience-centered formulations, there is another aspect of identity that requires attention: the adaptive or maladaptive revisions in the sense of self that emerge from life crises, stresses, and trauma, as well as the positive revisions that emerge through successful psychoanalysis. Furthermore, in our focus on being a doer doing, the sense of oneself as initiating and responding, activating and taking in, seeking, expecting, and fearing or avoiding all come into play. These "doings" lead to experiences of successes and agency or failure and powerlessness. How a person experiences success or failure entails disappointments in such endeavors and thus contributes to ongoing subtle shifts, adjustments, and adaptations in one's identity.

The way in which fractals can account for smooth shifts among the motivational systems also makes the concept ideally suited to capture the smooth shifts among self-states that characterize the therapeutic relationship. That relationship can be characterized as both partners having defined boundaries as well as open boundaries. Changes are thus promoted in the sense of self of both partners.

Therapeutic interactions continuously address or reflect diverse aspects of the patient's and therapist's sense of self. The patient's sense of self as worked on directly, but also to a large extent indirectly through growing sensitivity to the patient's underlying affect tone, can gradually alter, modify, and become more open to revision. When we speak of the affects, intentions, and goals of any dominant motivational system, we are simultaneously speaking of how we experience our self at that moment. Included in our sense of self is how we would like to be seen, how we try to seek to be seen, as well the possible tension between how we would like others to see us and how we feel we are being seen by them. Often painfully important is how we dread to be seen. When this aspect of the sense of self is dominant it is most difficult to tame in psychoanalytic treatment, as it was in the treatment of Eileen (below).

Clinical vignette

Eileen, in her late 30s, sought therapy with me (FML) because her life-long bouts of anxiety and panic attacks had only diminished slightly in her two previous treatments. Her explanation for her anxiety was that she had not found a mate and "time was running out" for her to have a child. In trying to diminish her anxiety, she became involved, repeatedly, with men with whom there was "no future." One man had been several years younger than she, and another man, although divorced, was still intricately involved with his ex-wife.

Eileen had certain crucial requirements with respect to the men with whom she became involved. These requirements were based predominantly on how she did not want to be seen and how she did not want to feel. Eileen is poised and attractive but – and this was for her a big "but" – she is six feet one inch tall. She feels ungainly and unlike the cute little girls whose appearance she envied in her childhood. To diminish these feelings, a man must be as tall but preferably taller than she. That's a tall order. And there was another requirement: the man's income must be equal to or greater than hers.

At the time when she began her treatment, both of these requirements appeared to have been based on how Eileen did not want to feel about herself or be seen by others. She did not want to tower over a man and feel ungainly, and she did not want a man to be less financially solvent than she was. That would make her the breadwinner, which had reverberations in her history. In addition, if the man's income was less than hers, it might appear to others as though she had to make concessions in order to land a man.

When Eileen met a man who came close to fulfilling her requirements, she would quite quickly live with him, and cling to him. Her sense of desperation came through in her description. The relationship would soon be over. Although in her descriptions of the relationships the outcome was quite obvious, when the ending did come it was always a surprise to her. These experiences of disillusion, recounted during our initial sessions, enabled us to get some sense of the current sources of her anxiety.

In sharp contrast to her chaotic early life, Eileen is well groomed. She grew up in an economically marginal family where clothing was hand-me-down. She called her mother "an aging hippie" who tried to support the family through menial work and part-time prostitution.

Her father was a "brutal-looking alcoholic" who abandoned the family shortly after the birth of Eileen's younger sister when Eileen was about 6 years old. She also has an older sister. Her mother was generally overwhelmed by having to raise three daughters on her own. Eileen described her home as being devoid of rules or structure. Most importantly, they never had enough money to provide for even basic necessities, such as clothing and cleaning supplies. This history contained the raw material that defined what she was seeking but, notably, also defined what she was seeking desperately to avoid. She sought a relationship that would conceal her "sordid" background and provide her with an identity that she had sought since childhood: to be a cute girl living in a clean, affluent home with a family that she and her husband (when she acquired one) would take care of. She dreaded recreating her childhood life and sought a life that would conceal the circumstances under which she had grown up. Yet, these intentions and goals made her feel like a fraud.

Eileen became a physician and she clearly did not have an income problem, but that was irrelevant. She believed that finding a man whose earnings were greater than hers would fill the void with which she had lived since childhood. Furthermore, although she liked her work, she wanted to feel she did not have to work.

Being so tall brought with it a sense of shame. She and her sisters, who were also tall but not as tall as she, had to wear the hand-me-down clothes of their cousins. As the tallest, Eileen had to wear the discarded clothes of her male cousin. Ever since her school days, when she had felt like an ungainly, sloppy boy, she longed to feel like a cute little girl.

Given the economics of her home, Eileen and her sisters had to work from the age of 13 on. At first Eileen helped her mother with cleaning jobs, but later she worked as a waitress at a restaurant in the mall near her home. An outlet store for women's clothing was next to that restaurant so Eileen was constantly confronted by young girls, with money, buying the cutest outfits. These girls made their way into Eileen's identity. They symbolized what did Eileen wanted to be. Therefore, finding a man who was as tall or even taller would be as close as she could get to looking cute and not so ungainly.

Standing in her messy, neglected home, amid the litter dropped by five cats, Eileen's mother impressed upon her that she could become anything that she wanted. That became a crucial mantra for Eileen. Of course, her mother was not aware then that what Eileen most wanted to become was a cute little girl with money.

Eileen and I considered that she may have felt enormously encouraged and supported by her mother's spirit. But it was particularly striking that neither through example nor action did her mother do anything to help her daughter articulate, approach, and try to achieve her goals. Yet she did instill in her daughters a desire to seek a better life. Through hard work, scholarships, and evidently enormous motivation focused predominantly on mastering her environment and gaining the symbols of prestige and respect, Eileen eventually succeeded in going to medical school and becoming a gynecologist. Alas, in important ways her success did little to alter her underlying affect tone of shame and fear of exposure to humiliation.

With respect to the three developmental pathways, Eileen's experience of intimacy in her home was suffused with garbage. Relationships among the three sisters and with their mother were dominated by the limitations that poverty imposes and the physical neglect with which they all lived. Intimacy was a luxury that was in short supply in Eileen's developing years. Eileen "escaped" by focusing on her school work and her determination to find a rescuer. With some feelings of resentment, she developed the skills to rescue herself through her intelligence and concentrated effort. Nevertheless, in spite of her diligent self-sufficiency, many overt achievements, and evident successes, Eileen felt that she was a fraud. It was as though she had breathed in the dust of shame that covered all aspects of her home and lived in dread that the filth and neglect would be discovered. Suffused with shame, despite her admirable appearance she considered herself to be a fraud.

As Eileen and I investigated the context and sources of this shame, we formulated a theme that connected several of her anxieties. She felt she had to carefully and thoroughly conceal her sordid family background, but doing so was exactly what made her feel fraudulent. She thereby opened herself up to being exposed as an impostor. The anxiety she felt was based on both her dread that her biological clock was ticking away and her equally powerful fear of being exposed. Then her embarrassing history of physical and emotional neglect – and perhaps even abuse – would be revealed. Those revelations would distinguish her from the other girls in her classes in school. Furthermore, her sense that she was not like any of the other girls in her grade school classes stretched even into her medical school classes. There, she felt herself to be an ungainly, boyish, dirty child. These were the repetitive patterns (fractals) that defined her sense of self. But, the boundaries were not open. The underlying affect tone of shame and fear of exposure remained unaffected, but the boundaries were not open. Eileen's numerous contrary experiences were devalued and prevented from being assimilated into her sense of self. These included the professional respect she had earned. Her dread of being seen constituted a major source of the anxiety for which she sought therapy while in medical school. Unfortunately, in her therapy in medical school, her anxiety was linked to a fear of failure in school, rather than her fear of being exposed, and so the anxiety persisted. While her success in school and in her career resulted in a degree of greater self-respect, her goal of eradicating her sordid background and becoming "a cute little girl" remained elusive.

The discrepancy between her mother's encouraging "you can be anything that you want to be" and her mother's life and actions served as an early source of dread about being exposed. It also defined an unbridgeable schism in her development of an identity. The mother who provided her with encouraging words simultaneously pulled the rug out from under her with her actions – or, rather, her lack thereof. Eileen's later and ongoing anxiety mirrored both the feeling of fraudulence and, as we were able to infer in our therapeutic work, the ever-present instability of the home in which she grew up.

Eileen's treatment focused to a large extent on the difference between how she saw herself, how she feared she would be seen, and how she wished to see herself and to be seen. In her desire to avoid exposure she felt compelled to downgrade the significance of experiences that could support her striving, more ambitious, and capable self. Such acceptance would only add fuel to the fires of her shame and sense of being a fraud. We attempted to untangle her mother's encouragement of seeking success from the visible evidence that her mother had surrendered to poverty. In doing so, she left her daughter alone in trying to extricate herself from the burden that her home life imposed on her. Spelling out these conflicting themes and their devastating effect on her implicitly moved Eileen toward engaging and loosening the boundaries between these diverse senses of herself. We recognized and articulated Eileen's dilemma to protect her mother that interfered with her assimilating her success and achievements into an identity that acknowledged and dominated her being a child of chaos. She felt the childhood picture of her chaos was real and any attempt to conceal it or "pretend" it was not so, as her sisters did, would be fraudulent.

The discrepancy between her mother's encouraging "you can be anything that you want" and her mother's life of failures was jarring, As her mother was encouraging academic success and achievements, she was surrounded by her three ill-cared-for children in their ramshackle squalid, chaotic house, dressed in the soiled, torn, worn-out, hand-me-down clothes donated by assorted male cousins

Eileen's sense of herself and underlying affect tone was organized through the sensory, visual, auditory, olfactory, and proprioceptive experiences that accumulated and impacted her during her formative years. Her professional choice of gynecology, after her youth dressed in shabby men's clothing, I imagine, gave her a hands-on sense of the female body and thus might provide reassurance as to her own femininity (we spelled this out as "They, women, are like me and I am like them. We are women and that's how I know I am not a man; I am a woman.") We spoke about her career choice in the context of her liking the women who trained and taught her ("a new mentoring family"), and she had felt comfortable in that assignment. Furthermore, she was now well respected at the hospital with which she was affiliated and had good relationships with the interns she trained. Eileen did not bring up her work as a problem area, but rather as an aspect of her life that had incorporated her mother's support and her own awareness that she was very smart. To go to college on academic and hardship scholarships and then to medical school required considerable work. She encountered no problems in her intellectual pursuits; however, her social life in college was problematic and she had her first experience with therapy there. Her relationship problems were evident by then and were addressed on a rather superficial level. She felt supported by her therapist but her anxiety remained. As mentioned earlier, she tried therapy in medical school because of her relationship problems and anxiety. What she was seeking in therapy, then as now, had not been recognized.

When Eileen and I discussed her previous treatment, we could see that her relationship problems could be understood better as manifestations of her shame-dominated sense of self and her fear that she would betray her sordid home life and upbringing and reveal the squalor and poverty from which she sprang.

Eileen and I articulated that what she wanted was a cleansing of her sordid background so that she would be freed of the shame it engendered. I said to her that what she could take with her from her home was her enormous capability to overcome significant obstacles and imposed limitations, and she could feel success in spite of the restrictions imposed by her family upbringing. We spoke about the strengths and resources she had developed, and I thought that these qualities were largely unrecognized by her. She was reluctant to accept these qualities as hers lest, by doing so, they would become tarnished by her background. We then were able to link her not crediting her achievements with her dread and conviction that she was a fraud.

Although Eileen had become the best-functioning member of her family, her older sister, who was not quite as tall as Eileen, had found a wealthy man whom, according to Eileen, "she exploits and who supports her." Eileen was still, after many years, profoundly envious of her. She said she would gladly trade places with her. Eileen admitted quite sheepishly that she wanted a man who was wealthier than her sister's boyfriend. Her younger sister has been lost to the world of drugs and in that sense is estranged from the family.

Eileen considered her height to be one of her deficits. She recalled that during her adolescence she eyed the cute, feminine-looking girls enviously. An obsessive doubting about her femininity ensued. These doubts most likely had earlier roots but were reinforced during this time. To conceal her shame and doubts, Eileen developed highly skilled compulsive and competitive patterns to be the best and to leave no opening for exposure or criticism. However, these patterns, while contributing to her academic success, never sufficed to squelch anxiety about being exposed and shamed, the affect down pull of her underlying shame ridden affect.

As we explored her relationships with men, Eileen told me that when she found a man who earned more money than her and was also taller than her, only then would she feel that she had been freed from the chaotic home of her childhood. Being rescued from her home and provided with a context that concealed her origins not only applied to money but to her "size" as well.

In an early session Eileen reported a dream. She was in her childhood home and there was a tiny man, more like a cute boy, dressed in a sailor's suit. With some embarrassment she said she was sure it was me. Although she had quite quickly formed an open and trusting relationship with me, there was a problem. She is much taller than me. She needed a man to make her feel "cute and feminine," and, because of my size, that was not me.

Being short had been an issue for me in my adolescence. My best friend was about 6 feet tall. (We became friends because we were both stamp collectors.) When we went to dances or parties together, we implicitly understood that the tall girls were for him and the short ones for me. When the tall ones were particularly good looking, I regretted my shortness and felt jealous. Although I have now come to accept my size, Eileen reminded me of those adolescent days and the feeling of inferiority over my height. More than sensing into her state of mind as an observer, I shared her sense of fragile self-worth. In contrast, that I now had one of these very tall, good-looking women sitting opposite was not lost on me. I did not have to relinquish her to my tall friend – who, coincidentally, had become an analyst.

Eileen believed she needed a man to make her feel "cute and feminine," and she feared that was not going to be me. To emphasize the serious nature of her problem, she then described her shame at wearing the old clothes of male cousins. Even now she needed to buy some clothes and shoes from the men's department of stores. The size requirement for a mate was nonnegotiable, she told me. I said to her that she could certainly decide on the shape of man to whom she is attracted, but at this point needing someone to be taller than herself might be linked to her doubts about her femininity and that is something that we might explore further. We also investigated her fear that my being short might not work in rescuing her from the chaos of her childhood. Was she engaged in yet another unsuccessful therapeutic attempt to fulfill her expectations? We addressed this concern by focusing on the numerous resources and persistent motivations that have enabled her to succeed and transcend her background.

Motivations to explore and master were trounced by aversiveness: not to be like her mother and reproduce her mother's failures. We also explored how Eileen had come to organize her identity but failed to include her intellectual abilities and ambitions. She had teachers all through grade school and high school who gave substance to her mother's statement that "you can do anything that you want." Or, put differently, she sought out teachers whom she admired and who offered to help her develop the skills she needed to fulfill her ambitions. Medical school became a goal in her high school years, abetted by her watching television programs that took place in hospitals where, she explained to me, the doctors were always "scrubbing up." I observed that it served as the ideal profession through which to rid herself of the accumulated grime of her childhood home. Yet no amount of medical school scrubbing had, as yet, made a dent in the chaos of her home life.

There was another element in this dream that led to a number of different themes: the sailor suit. These suits were typically worn by young boys from the wealthier homes who went to Eileen's school. They were the boys who would grow up to date and become the partners of the cure little girls that she envied. These boys were in another league, and she would never be in their league. We were able to address one transference question: whether I, or anyone who had not lived in her home, could ever understand her. She feared that this was another unbridgeable gulf between us (in addition to the difference in our sizes). She feared this alienated her from becoming part of the community of cute people. Recognizing and articulating these fears was all that was required for Eileen to feel that I, one of the cute but as yet unattainable people, understood her dread.

An interpretation that she was attempting to "belittle" me, or an expression of her envy of me, did not fit well into the spirit of the session at that time. Although such an unconscious message cannot be ruled out, the more direct message, contextualized, was that she typically felt herself to be ungainly, not feminine, and exposed, for all the world to see her shameful and sordid background. In this way she communicated to me the issue that had not received sufficient recognition in her two previous treatments and the aspect of her sense of self she wanted us to address.

In those treatments, utilizing interpretation and insight, Eileen's underlying feeling state of being trapped in unmodifiable shame had not been engaged. Perhaps my being short was a blessing in disguise in Eileen's treatment. It crystallized her somewhat vague, but persistent pessimistic self-state in the therapeutic ambiance. It became manifest and directly engaged in our transference–countertransference. Thus, my recognition and articulation of this issue directly impacted Eileen's experience of herself in relation to me and fed into a gradual increased sense of hopeful possibility both in her conscious awareness and her underlying affect tone of pessimism and shame.

But there was more. There was yet another aspect to the sailor suit. Some of the men her mother brought home were sailors. For Eileen, sailors were men who were here today and gone tomorrow. The sailor suit thus also referred to the unpredictability and the unreliability of men, beginning with her father who abandoned the family. The sailor suit covered the instability of the world in which Eileen grew up.

As we explicated these various themes, the underlying ambiance with which Eileen had lived became clearer. I spelled it out as

there is nothing firm, nothing I can count on. I have to find someone who can provide that for me or I have to provide it for myself. But anyone who could provide me with that stability is out of my league. So that is hopeless.

These diverse feelings added up to the underlying anxious tone that Eileen brought into her social relationships and her therapies.

As we articulated what had been the ever-present underlying ambiance that provided a backdrop for Eileen's experience, her view of herself gradually shifted. Her clouds of identity began to come together to form a new cloud. Spelling out the myriad of feelings that Eileen had retained from her childhood experience and her determination to find a life for herself that would both conceal and eradicate that experience were reconfigured as these were my experiences and challenges. I have worked hard and succeeded in making a better world for myself than the one in which she grew up. Thereby Eileen could begin to access experiences that contained her resources and strengths, experiences that had previously been denied access to her self-organization.

Eileen was also determined not to follow the example of her sisters, who pretended not to notice their surroundings, the squalor of their home. She was determined not to exclude what her sisters were determined to pretend did not exist. Her younger sister lived in a world dominated by her drug addiction, and her older sister with the "rich" boyfriend looked down on her family as though she had never been part of it. Eileen prided herself on being truthful and not "pretending." But doing so came at a price. When we explored what prevented her from including the resources and abilities that she possessed, she brought up another dream image:

> I hung my white coat [the one she wears at the hospital] on a hook in the closet at the hospital where I always hang it. My coat dropped to the floor and fell on the winter boots there. It got all dirty splattered with snow and mud.

The dream sounded an alarm. Keep your professional life away from the dirt of the outside world; it will sully what you have achieved. She needed to keep her resources apart from her history lest, by including these strengths, they could become tarnished with the messes of her childhood home. By keeping her academic and professional accomplishments apart from her sense of self that remained organized by her childhood shame she attempted to keep her resources unsullied by a past that left her shame ridden.

Shortly after the session in which we worked on the meaning that integrating her resources with the sense of self derived from her childhood, Eileen arrived for a session in a very, very revealing blouse. I was in a dilemma now. I did not want to embarrass her or make her feel self-conscious, but I also did not want to ignore this nonverbal but obvious communication to me. I gave her an obvious affectionate smile, laced, with just a touch of lust. She smiled back at me. And that was it.

In the course of the session that followed, Eileen indicated that she was not going anywhere special after the session, suggesting that the blouse was meant for me. I heard this as her appreciating that I responded as subtly as I did. She was also signaling me that the blouse represented some pride and acceptance of her feminine and erotic sense of self. And, indeed, I could see that she was showing me a fractal of much that she was proud of.

Looking back on Eileen's therapy, bringing these divergent and until then bounded aspects of her sense of self together – the childhood history and home life, the professional and academic world in which she also thrived, and her sense that she was proud of her physical appearance – resembled the merging of the cloud formations that were bounded as well as possessing open boundaries.

At long last Eileen could also begin to feel a sense of pride in her achievements, struggles, and accomplishments without fearing that they would be tarnished in the process

In our work on this shift, we continuously came up against Eileen's fear that she would be thrust back into her childhood world and lose her accomplishments. In this fear we recognized that she had actually now begun to value her achievements and that the newly organized sense of self had begun to absorb her past and recent achievements and strengths. I said to Eileen that you can't worry about losing something that you don't think you have.

Eileen's sense of herself was co-constructed in the context of our dialogue. Her trust that I saw her – the competent doctor, the attractive woman with a sensual body – and not her sordid past led to a shift in ambiance between us from pessimism to hopefulness and trust. We brought together images and recollections that appeared in different sessions as well as from different times in her life: the rag-like clothes and the unkempt home of her early childhood, the "encouragement" from her mother echoed by her teachers from her puberty years, as well as her ambitions and intellectual resources that she had disregarded both to protect them and not to join her sisters since she considered them as demonstrating her fraudulence. The spirit between us gradually took on a joint quality of seeking, of inquiry, of shared feelings (twinship) that was reflected and responsible for shifting the underlying affect tone from shame to pride and from pessimism to optimism.

One's identity, like one's sense of self, is organized along a temporal dimension. By bridging past and present experiences and future expectations, Eileen integrated previously sequestered experiences that reflected aspects of herself that could accrue to a cohesive sense of self. Furthermore, this integration enabled us to understand the image of the tiny analyst figure as a depiction of Eileen's self-consciousness about being so tall and her longing from childhood to be one of the cute, cared-for girls. The image contained both her fear that I would not be big enough to help her as well as her wish to become a "small and cute" person as she had always wished she could be. Perhaps the "cute" analyst could help her become a "cute" patient? At the end, she felt the cute analyst could accept her as a tall woman, and that she had not been feeling like an ungainly boy was revealed by her blouse.

References

Jaobson, E. (1967) *The self and the object world*. Madison, Ct.: International Universities Press.

Lichtenberg, J., Lachmann, F. and Fosshage, J. (2011) *Psychoanalysis and motivational systems: A new look*. New York, NY: Routledge.

Chapter 3

The treatment of Samantha

In Chapter 1 we hypothesized and cited considerable evidence in support of how *seeking* fundamentally provides the spark to activate the various intentions and goals framed in our seven motivational systems. Seeking begins in utero, expands more fully within the neonate, and continues in increasing complexity throughout life. Without the spark of seeking we would become inert, lifeless, without desire or intention. A sense of agency, a sense of a doer doing, would be undermined and the affective tone would be predominantly depressed.

How does seeking become strengthened or undermined in one's life? Positive, successful experience reinforces and strengthens the spark of seeking more generally as well as, more specifically, activating particular motivation(s). Successful experience establishes positive expectancies that, in turn, reinforce seeking and enhance vitality. In contrast, negative, failing or unsuccessful experiences undermine seeking as well as the specific activated motivation, and establish or reinforce negative expectancies.

In this chapter we highlight clinical material that involves the three broad developmental pathways delineated in Chapter 1: 1) the pathway for human relatedness and intimacy; 2) the pathway for mastering the environment; and 3) the pathway for a healthy body, physiological regulation, and a good mind–body connection. In addition, we described in Chapter 1 how particular underlying generalized affect tones become established, beginning early in life, on the basis of lived intersubjective or relational experience.

When a person makes a call for psychoanalytic treatment, it is a resilient, hopeful spark to seek once again the needed ingredients for connection, self-esteem, a sense of agency, and hope that we can achieve our intentions and goals. Each of the protagonists in the analytic relationship enter with his/her respective subjectivities and underlying generalized affect tones, co-creating specific ambiances in the patient/analyst process. These ambiances at times can be worked on explicitly, expanding *reflective awareness* of the underlying affect tones and their current and past relational experiential origins – a gradual transformative process. In addition, psychoanalytic change requires *new relational experience* within and outside of the analytic relationship that occurs both at explicit and implicit levels, to establish more positive affect tones and vitalizing expectancies.

In our book, *Enlivening the Self* (2016), I (JLF) presented the psychoanalytic story of Samantha in chapter 2, "Clinical Guidelines." We illustrated the developmental processes that occurred over the course of a 15-year psychoanalysis. We now represent the clinical material to highlight change processes occurring more specifically along the three developmental pathways described in Chapter 1: that is, human relatedness and intimacy, mastering the environment, and physiological regulation. We will feature how these change processes are brought about through expanding empathically based reflective awareness (i.e., the explicit reflective/exploratory/understanding) and through cocreating other new implicit and explicit relational processes. We highlight, in particular, the change in Samantha's underlying generalized affect tones and change in the patient/analyst's cocreated analytic ambiances. We point out the dominant, as well as changes in, affect tones as Samantha in her waking life and in her dream-life attempts to overcome the considerable trauma that had been so disruptive for her.

As the therapy unfolds, we will attempt to recognize and evaluate progress in understanding the problematic organizing themes and their origins, enhancing current successful adaptive patterns, and forming new capacities emerging out of new lived experience. Has the patient become more resilient in responding to a disruption? Has the therapist become more able to recognize disruptions and better able to discern their source, in terms of both the patient's and his contribution? Do therapist and patient feel increasingly known by each other, especially as each relates to the other in their interactions? Is there an increased understanding of the activation of various problematic self-states with corresponding affect tones and capacity to deactivate these states? Has a new interactive pattern emerged with a new, more adaptive authenticity of each, enhancing a sense of doers doing? Has the dyad been able to engage within a social context that has become more flexible and enlivened? Does a favorable old pattern or a newly formed one open patient and therapist to increased experiences of feeling deeply touched? Are there moments of admiration of the sensibility and exploratory skills of one another and both together? Have negative attributions become replaced by new attributions more accurately reflecting the essential strivings of each and of their joint efforts?

As we present a psychoanalytic case study, we address each of the developmental processes for their relevance in understanding and facilitating therapeutic change. While the case was treated by one of us (JLF), discussions of it in the "comments" attached to the narrative reflect our common understanding.

A wintry village

I (Fosshage, 1999) have selected an analysand and an analytic process transpiring over a course of 15 years and intermittently over another 5 years. More than 25 years ago, I received a phone call from a male analyst colleague. I will call him Jay. I did not know him well. He was a man in his early 60s. In my brief exposure to him, I had experienced him as bright, outspoken, and argumentative. Jay told me that he had fallen in love with an analysand of his. After consulting with his former analyst, he had decided to tell his analysand of his feelings for her and his desire for a social romantic relationship with her, and shortly thereafter had terminated the treatment. At his invitation, she began to live with him – four days after the termination. Three weeks later, they agreed that she needed an analyst and I received the call. Recognizing that this was a highly unusual and problematic situation, Jay, implicitly expressing his trust in me, inquired if I would be willing to see her in light of these circumstances. I told him that I would see her and suggested that she call me. He informed me that she was right there and put her on the phone. With a clear voice, she expressed in an enthusiastic and straightforward manner her desire to see me, whereupon we scheduled an appointment.

> _Comment:_ "With a clear voice, she expressed in an enthusiastic and straightforward manner her desire to see me" represented what I came to understand to be one dominant underlying affect state of Samantha. In this instance she was feeling hopeful and enthusiastic about seeking psychotherapeutic help._

Several days later, I saw Samantha. Samantha, a woman of 37, spoke well, was quite attractive, dressed in a casual, trendy manner, and demonstrated a charm and outspokenness. Her outspokenness, however, carried a tension that I sensed was part of her battle to overcome what had been experienced as squelching influences. Her mood was quite elevated. She was "flying high" and clearly in the thrall of an idealizing love of her former analyst/ now boyfriend. I sensed that her elevated mood was not only related to the initial stages of "being in love," which commonly includes a mutual self-enhancing idealization, but also to a somewhat strained, yet valiant effort to overcome anticipated criticism as well as, perhaps, ambivalent feelings of her own. I liked her, felt interested and engaged, and wondered where our work would take us.

> *Comment:* *"I" refers to the analyst and principal author here and "we" refers to the three authors of the book commenting, highlighting the implications for the three developmental pathways, underlying affect tones, and analytic ambiances that we are illustrating. I responded to Samantha's enthusiasm with my own enthusiasm, cocreating a dyadic ambiance of liking each other, of mutual interest in one another, and of a mutual anticipation that we could work successfully with each other.*

Samantha's first treatment experience, she explained, occurred some years back when she was going through marital difficulties and, subsequently, a divorce. She had married in her early twenties and divorced three years later. Her therapist was a "Freudian analyst" who had known her family. She critically described him as "cerebral, un-empathic, detached, and un-nurturing" – what I took as warning signals of what I should not be, and most probably, I thought, resonated with previous trauma. Experiencing the analyst as too close to her family and too removed to trust, she ended up "manipulating him in orchestrating the sessions to amuse him and to avoid certain areas." Terminating after two years, she exclaimed to me, "I was fucked by him," for she felt "blamed by him" and ended up feeling worse.

Approximately ten years later she sought treatment with Jay. At that time she was feeling profoundly depressed and periodically suicidal – what I subsequently realized was another *underlying affect state*, that is, a self-state dominated by conflict, anxiety, and depression, including negative views of herself, fury, and hopelessness. She said that she was conflicted "between what I was bred to be and my inner integral self...My inner self had been squashed and wants out or I will die…I was the perfect child – forget it – I am not the repressed, elegant Swiss-German girl." She had been taught "to control [her feelings] cerebrally." As a result, she felt "an Amazon woman in me emerging that was previously smashed." She had entered into analysis with Jay on a 4–5 times-a-week basis and began to take Prozac. The analysis lasted for six months.

> _Comment:_ In her initial session Samantha was clearly intent on emphatically describing how her parents had not seen or known her "inner integral self" (in our language, authentic self). Instead, her parents had imposed upon her their image of a "repressed, elegant Swiss-German girl." To maintain the attachment and secure affirmation, Samantha pathologically accommodated (Brandchaft et al., 2010) to her parents' attributions and requirements to become "the perfect child"; yet, she was quite aware of an intense defiance – that is, "an Amazon woman" ready to emerge within her. This psychological battle between accommodating or fighting her parents' attributions intensified Samantha's aggressive affect tone of rebellion and defiance. Her parents were quite successful, especially her father, which required defiance in an effort to claim herself. The family battle, along with her parents' excessive expectations, undoubtedly encumbered her efforts to establish a career that belonged to her.

Based on her report, Samantha quickly became intensely engaged in the analytic work with Jay, fostered by her feeling deeply understood for the first time in her life. With the establishment of an idealizing and mirroring selfobject connection, her spirits lifted and medication was discontinued. Clearly the analysis had gone well until the analyst's needs more directly entered the scene. She described how they had become very close, expressing their affection for one another. She recalled hugs at the end of the session, initiated by Jay. His occasionally giving her a ride home after a late-night session was somewhat confusing, yet it was experienced as part of an increasing closeness. Jay, who had been divorced for some time, then told her that he loved her and that he wanted to stop treatment and marry her. She responded positively, for she had never felt so understood or deeply connected to a man. They terminated the analysis and, very shortly thereafter, were engaged to be married.

Samantha and I had connected easily during the first session. Although I was well aware of Jay's breach of ethics, I was most concerned about Samantha's welfare. I did not report Jay, for it would have precluded Samantha's analysis. I knew that Jay's analyst was informed and carried the ethical responsibility. My priority was to protect a safe space for Samantha's analysis. I decided not to express concern to Samantha about what had happened. Samantha was "in love." Any hint of concern, I felt, would have evoked aversion in her in the service of protecting her love connection with Jay, foreclosing self-reflection and the expression of other feelings. I overcame temptations to prejudge the situation by reminding myself that I did not really "know" whether her relationship with Jay might work, as on rare occasions such relationships have succeeded. I believe that my openness to this possibility facilitated my listening closely to Samantha's experience and to *her* feelings and assessments – that is, to listen from within an empathic perspective – that helped her "find" herself.

> <u>Comment</u>: *In light of what she had already said about a core conflict between her integral self and how she was bred, which left her authentic self unrecognized, I was quite aware of not wanting to impose on her yet still another judgment and agenda. In addition, "to know" another person requires understanding from within the other person's perspective (empathic listening), and at the moment she was "in love," despite the problematic context.*

Based on her initiative, we decided to meet on a twice-weekly basis, because, in addition to financial limitations, I believe we both felt that she did not want to jump quickly into yet another intense analytic relationship.

During the next session Samantha spoke about how her older brother had been killed in a car accident more than twenty years earlier. She was the only remaining child. Nevertheless, she focused primarily on her relationship with Jay and how her parents were distressed about him. Samantha described her parents as "cerebral, controlled, intellectual, and scared." Her father had sarcastically quipped, "A patient marries her therapist, every woman's dream!" He saw her as an "invalid daughter" who needed to be taken care of by a man – a powerful, disparaging parental attribution. Her mother was also critical and gave Jay what Samantha described as "a manipulative dose" during their first meeting, saying "You must have a pick of all your patients." Samantha was, unfortunately, all too familiar with these undermining comments in the face of "bad behavior." Shaken by her parents' skepticism, it became even more imperative that she hold steadfast to her love and commitment to Jay.

Over the next six weeks, Samantha spoke about her inner experience, especially using her dreams and imagistic symbolic processing to create a narrative and deal with intense, dramatic conflict. What could not find explicit expression without jeopardizing her parental connections, her fragile state of mind, and her efforts to express and regulate her affects, erupted in her dream life. The first dream she reported, after four weeks of treatment, was as follows:

> I'm an oriental woman; her skin is white, her hair dark, wearing no clothes. The sky is pale – it's very quiet. There's a big dune with white, fine sand. I was at the crescent of the dune to see the ocean – one place I have peace. At the bottom of the dune were two oriental children – small; they were dead. They were laid out on their stomachs facing the ocean. They had died because they had been thrashed on their backs with a huge bouquet of small pink roses. I had also been thrashed on my back.
>
> I repeatedly went up to the crescent of the dune to see. The children changed. One time it was me and my brother – one time, my parents. I'm hurting them in my will to grow.
>
> [She comments outside the dream] I did not intend to hurt others. Sometimes they were my children that I never had. I woke up with my body taut, like there were vultures going to pick my bones.

In our ensuing discussion, Samantha mentioned how, at one point during the previous Fall, she was feeling deeply suicidal; she developed a welt on her back and had a dream that her mother had put a knife in her back. Here, in this dream, the pink roses delivered the fatal blows. "Flowers were given in the name of love," she described, "but they persistently killed me, brutalized me, controlled me. They did something so beautiful but deadly." She spoke of two sides of herself: "What I was bred to be and what I am inside…I can't bring the two together." For her, to grow, to live from the inside out rather than from the outside in, was tantamount to hurting, even killing her parents for they had been so invested in creating a child in their image. She could find moments of peace fully exposed at the "crescent" of the dune overlooking the ocean, but below her lay the small dead children who had been killed. She ends up terrified of vultures. Retrospectively viewed, these core issues framed much of what was to come.

> <u>Comment</u>: *Gradually, Samantha's life story unfolded during these first few weeks, but in an unusually piecemeal fashion. Her elaborate dreams would often bring up pieces that would then be filled out. While highly articulate in person, her waking narrative about herself had not yet become all that coherent. It was full of dissociated fragments. Her intense conflict between her own perceptual, affective, cognitive experience – that was "her" and could serve as a self anchor – and her parents' imperious expectations and wishes interfered with her striving for and consolidating a more cohesive, authentic sense of self. Consumed with these conflicts, and her parents with theirs, Samantha's relational experience had not created the needed space and inner quiet to reflect, nor to form and articulate a more coherent picture of her life. Hence, even the following brief summary could only be constructed over a considerable period of time. I believe that her own narrative had been disrupted by her parent's imposition of their narrative, which was replete with attributions that were either denigrating or full of grand expectations.*
>
> *Her parents' grand expectations were intimidating and left her prone to feel insufficient, a failure.*
>
> *When Samantha accommodated her parents, she would become momentarily depressed with feelings of capitulation, of losing herself, of "badness," and hopelessness about impacting her parents – a self-state with underlying affects that would take over. With increased understanding of her upset, she felt fortified and would resiliently reassert herself.*

Samantha's father was highly successful in the arts and her mother was well educated, musical, and worked in publishing. Swiss–German in origin, they raised their family with strong interests in education, music, and culture, and strong values for hard work, compunction, and dedication. Rules, regulations, and achievement were the order of the day. Samantha often experienced her mother as hysterically and intensely talking above her and at her. Her mother's quick temper and rages emerged a bit later in treatment. Samantha portrayed her mother and father as tense and busy people who insisted that things were to be done "right." While tension was often in the air and expressed loudly, there was little room for reflectively relating emotional experience.

Analytic sessions became the place where she could express herself, aggressively assert herself, and find the necessary reflective, calm space to articulate herself.

> _Comment_: In the family, fighting was routine between parents, between parent and child, and between children. Disruptions were not reflectively talked about and resolved in the family. Instead, self-injuries triggered rage that, in turn, undermined possible repair. Similar to their parents, Samantha and her brother, older by four years, fought intensely. Unable to open up the emotional tension to ferret out its meaning, her father finally nailed shut the door that adjoined their two rooms.

Samantha had experienced her family as ricocheted with tensions; yet, she had pride in her family. She was raised to be the perfect model child, the elegant young woman. While success on this front fostered the development of some confidence in her intelligence, attractiveness, and style, she seemed to realize that, in response to her parents' powerful agenda, she had been forced to subjugate all too much of her own perceptual and affective experience. She continued to wage a terrible battle between "who I was bred to be and who I am inside."

> _Comment_: While her parents' anxieties and impositions interfered with Samantha's desired development of a successful intimate relationship and interfered with her career pursuits, her parents' intelligence, success in the arts, and style certainly contributed to Samantha's artistic style and interpersonal confidence. Her parents' work ethic and success in the arts also opened up areas of interest and kindled ambitious desires and plans. Samantha first developed as a serious ballet dancer and later turned to writing as a career. So, the arts ran strongly within her and her family. Her parents' expectations, judgments, self-focus, and the loss of a young adult child played havoc with her establishing her career (pathway for mastering the environment). Initially through ballet dance and, later, through focused exercise, Samantha has always been attentive to physical care and regulation.

A major tragedy befell her family when her brother was killed in a car accident in his mid-twenties. Her parents dealt with the tragedy by shutting down emotionally. They did not talk about her brother. It was as if he had never existed. Soon thereafter, they sold their beloved beach home where, for many years, and close to nature, they had lived more fully as a family. The loss of her brother, the further loss of emotional connection to her parents, and the loss of the valued beach home wreaked emotional havoc in Samantha.

Comment: While Samantha's parents had accomplished and created a cultured family with considerable positive experience, they had great difficulty in dealing with emotional tensions and traumatic losses. At those times, anxiety, tension, and rage dominated the scene (that is, a low threshold for negative affects had been established) with scarce resources for reflective processing. The underlying affective tone was a deep anxiety that life was overwhelming and overtaxing. Samantha would often feel taken over by this anxiety. As we understood its source, the analytic sessions served to create the needed calm and reassurance that the issues could be managed. Analysis became a much-needed reflective harbor.

Her dreams, long and complex narratives, were often desperate attempts at trying to deal with these traumatic losses. A small portion of her second dream clearly tells the story:

I am at the age I was then, but also now. We are selling the house. A couple comes to see it. It is very important to me that they are a couple that understand the house. I don't think there is such a couple. D, T (my parents), and I have spent all this time getting the house in shape in order to sell it. All of our hearts are full of grief. Each one of us does not want to give up the house for our own reasons, but we cannot communicate to each other what those reasons are. We are each locked in our own grief and sadness and led by this pain to pass judgment on ourselves and each other. We stand in judgment on ourselves and assume the rest of the family will also. We proceed to follow the correct "form" of what apparently needs to be done: getting rid of the house that reminds T (mother) of my brother. We follow her lead because she is so unhappy and make the explanation that the house is too big to maintain and therefore must be sold.

Meanwhile, during the first two months of treatment, Samantha's relationship with Jay began to deteriorate. In contrast to the careful listening and understanding that had occurred in the analytic relationship, she began to experience him as controlling and demanding, with little regard for her wishes. She thought of herself as being a very sexual person; yet, she found Jay to be disrespectful and sexually controlling. He reacted to her objections and assertions with rage, which was all too reminiscent of her family. Samantha began to feel that she had given up too much of her life, a feeling that resonated deeply with themes of the past. She had a nightmare in which she was married to Frankenstein – it was Jay. She was trying to escape. In the dream, he and she were both malformed. Not only was this now her experience of Jay, it also reflected how for years she had thought that something was wrong with her. Now, in the ensuing throes of a rapid and unrelenting de-idealization, she began to see Jay as an older, lonely man who was desperately self-focused and controlling. Moreover, he was defensive and unable to reflect or talk about their deteriorating relationship. In turn, Samantha became horrified and ashamed about how she got into this situation. Recalling her analysis with him, she felt that when she had begun to express her sexual feelings, Jay had encouraged detailed elaboration of them. She realized that at times he had become sexually aroused. Subsequently, he began on occasion to respond with sexual overtones. She had responded in kind, which now horrified her. Yet, the ingredients of her response – feeling affirmed and understood, sexual excitement, intimacy, and capitulation – could still not really be assessed. Instead, her distrust and sense of betrayal, rage, and shame became increasingly intense. Within two months she had broken off the relationship, despite his angry protestations, and returned to her apartment.

Her experience of Jay's abusive imposition and betrayal resonated with experiences from her past. Gradually, it emerged that her brother had made sexual advances and a trusted neighbor had insistently come on to her as an adolescent. Physical abuse occurred with her mother who, in rage, would strike out at her, slapping her face and "beating the shit out" of her.

Comment: In her relationships with her parents a sense of betrayal in the form of criticism and the imposition of their agendas pervaded. Physical and sexual abuse repeated the theme of domination and not being seen. Compliance or defiance dominated the scene.

Over the next four months, Samantha felt increasingly angry at Jay's betrayal and manipulation of their trusting analytic relationship. She felt abused and victimized, and harbored deep shame about her involvement. She finally decided to sue him, which for her was an attempt to reassert herself, to impact him, to overcome the sense of victimization, to become a "doer." Her lawyer asked for my participation. In considering the potential repercussions of this with Samantha, not the least of which was the potential for the suit to dominate the analysis, I emphasized the importance of protecting our analytic relationship. I also knew that the analyst in the courtroom is easily discredited as biased, leaving little to be gained from my direct involvement. While I was well aware of the importance of my support of the suit for Samantha, with her agreement I declined to participate directly in it. Later, she expressed her gratitude. At her lawyer's request I referred Samantha to a psychiatrist who provided a psychiatric evaluation for the suit. After negotiations between the lawyers, Jay threatened violence against her and her attorney. Shortly thereafter, she agreed to a pretrial settlement with financial recompense, which provided some satisfaction along with a sense of retribution.

The experience with Jay had been traumatic, with considerable fallout, including destabilizing her trust of the analytic relationship. Could she really trust an analyst again? Could she trust a man again? She vowed never again to have sexual feelings for her analyst, which was clearly directed at me, for she felt that I, too, would be unable to contain them and would become stimulated and betray her. She felt threatened by an analyst's power as well as by her own seductive capacity. She wrote,

> I cannot accept that I allowed this to happen to me. I cannot understand that I was a victim. I cannot come to terms with my participation in this relationship…I feel violated, ashamed, revolted, helpless, sickened, furious, bereft, betrayed, abandoned, fucked, raped, abused, disgusted. I feel trapped by the trail of abuse and betrayal he has left in me. I feel unclean, unwhole, completely compromised. I cannot accept that I was helpless and powerless to act otherwise at the time.

While her compliance and victimization felt intolerable, her sexual response and active participation was equally unacceptable.

Comment: When distrust was in the foreground in the analytic relationship, I attempted to live in and explore her experience of the analytic relationship. We explored her experience, what we have referred to as the attributions of the transference (Lichtenberg, et al., 1996), to understand them in light of whatever triggers might have occurred between us. I understood her attributions to have been cocreated, through my contribution and through her anticipation or construction based on her lived experience in her previous analytic relationship and her parental and familial relationships.

Despite her wariness, Samantha appeared to experience me usually as protective and caring – hallmarks of an idealizing selfobject transference – which corresponded with how I felt toward her. She increasingly experienced me as "solid" in a way that helped to reassure her that our relationship would not get out of control, a fundamental prerequisite for our cocreation of a new relational experience where new expectations are learned. During this phase of the analysis, selfobject relatedness, for her, was in the foreground, and, for me, my "caretaking" or being concerned with her formed a reciprocal relationship (Fosshage, 1997) with her idealizing selfobject needs. This created a particular kind of closeness, similar to a father with a young daughter, that was satisfying to both of us. To experience me as a person who would have additional needs, however, was, at this juncture, a powerful trigger of terror. She dreaded that she would again be exposed to betrayal, domination, and abuse. Hence, her experience of me during this time, we learned, needed to be circumscribed around my "caretaking" efforts in order to cocreate the requisite safety and protectiveness.

> *Comment: Our consistent reflective processing of disruptions that were triggered within the analytic and outside relationships was creating a new procedure for reparation (through understanding the triggers and each other's contributions). It was also gradually lowering the threshold for positive experience and was deepening a fundamental cooperative, trusting connection (that is, trusting that I honored her initiative and was not attempting to impose my agenda or understandings on her).*

In the work arena, Samantha had given up a full-time position with a company in the arts where the corporate structure was experienced as oppressive and her boss was intrusive and controlling. She freelanced but struggled financially and suffered from a lack of career direction. She wanted to write but lacked confidence and had not been able to sustain a consistent effort.

In the course of the analytic process that ensued, Samantha began to deal with memories and with her affective life that had been frozen off (dissociated). Her dreams, which expressed her imagistic giftedness, were excruciatingly long and painful. As she wrote them, painful memories emerged. I have selected small portions of one dream that occurred approximately 14 months into treatment. The dream opens with Samantha on the beach watching the surfers play in the late afternoon. She must pick up her father and begins to worry that she will be late and be accused of being irresponsible. She writes:

> I am on my way again to my destination. However, I am angry and feel I am "behaving" obstreperously. The surfers have gone, but have left their surfboards behind, standing in tumbles next to the pier. I can see the fish hooks in the sand and the fishing poles beside them. The hooks stick out from the surface of the sand. I sit and look at them first, and then very decidedly walk towards them, all the do's and don't's and restrictions, regulations, controls, musts, have to's, shoulds, always, never to, and will now do's, given to me by my parents are ringing in my ears as I walk across the beach. I want to touch this dark blue surf board, it sits, fin facing me, the underbelly of it slightly worn down, the color rubbed slightly away from being pulled across the sand after being in the water. It's like a blue finned whale. I walk across the fish hooks and feel and hear the hooks puncturing my skin, and curving into it, and out on the other side. I don't care. I must reach out and touch that blue board. I feel the pain of the hooks, but am disembodied from it at the same time.

In her undaunted effort to touch the "blue surfboard" that reminds her of a "blue finned whale," she initially found it necessary to "disembody" herself from the pain of the impaling fishhooks. Later in the dream, she begins to feel the excruciating pain as she tries to free herself from the hooks. She knows that her parents will reprimand her. There is a concert that night, and she realizes that she has ruined their evening for they will need to take her to the hospital to have the hooks extracted. What stood out for us in our discussion was what placed her in jeopardy: her need to touch the blue board and to feel its beauty, despite the exposed fish hooks, and the need to defy her parents' agendas, constant admonitions, and prohibitions. Her parents would not be sympathetic; they would be furious with her, reigniting the desperate struggle to find, in spite of the danger and in defiant reaction against her parent's dictates, some beauty, some freedom, some peace as captured in the image of the dark blue surfboard. The blue surfboard was a powerful image for Samantha, capturing her desire for freedom of movement, for gliding with nature, for peaceful existence and beauty, as a way of creating a sense of agency and an enlivened affective experience. It was a solitary experience of enlivenment.

As she wrote this dream, traumatic memories burst into her awareness – having been hit by a car and then having been hit by her enraged mother; of being called to dinner, forcing her to leave her cat to die alone; of her broken arm, which her parents did not immediately take care of; of not being told the truth before she underwent dental surgery; of not being told of her brother's death for eight hours after he was killed; and of her father's screaming at her when she saw him naked when she was 11 years old – "the shame he made me feel."

> *Comment*: *Her intention and determination to reach the freedom of the surfboard, "her destination," still required painful, even dangerous, defiance of her parents' agenda. With the lessening of her dissociation, she was able to feel the pain more fully and to recall the traumatic memories. As long as the pain was completely frozen (dissociated) we had not been able to deal reflectively with the pain and integrate the trauma.*

Close variations of a dream, which had reoccurred over the previous 14 months, involved her checking her room before she and her parents leave the beach house after the sale. She finds the drawers and closets are full. She writes,

> Everything I own, memories signified by my belongings, tumble, tumble out into my arms. I am always the last. Everyone else is pulled together. My parents appeared, or have denied, not to have any difficulty in leaving. This time they are on the ferry line, and I sit overwhelmed in my room finding more and more things to take with me. I have already been chastised for having so many bags. The rest of the

house looks like a museum – I just wrote mausoleum. Only my room is chaotic or alive.

We understood that, on the one hand, she was laden with memories that needed to be sorted through, and, on the other hand, she was desperately trying to recapture and to hold on to the memories that could provide a sense of stability and self-continuity. Yet, in the face of her parents' denial, impatience, and fury, she always felt in a panic. Panic became another underlying affect state – panic that her parents clearly experienced and were overwhelmed with. Samantha felt that she did not have the time or the parental help to sort through her belongings one by one, to assess, to reflect, to tarry, to keep them with her or to discard as she desired.

As Samantha dissociated less, her inner world of intense conflict and painful memories emerged more fully, at times becoming excruciatingly terrifying. She experienced powerful urges to jump out her 10th-floor apartment window, which we came to understand was jumping out to "freedom," free of the expectations, the restrictions, the inner turmoil. She became terrified, and I became deeply concerned that, at the height of pain, she might impulsively go for this last-ditch effort to end the intense suffering. Medication was prescribed, but the terrors of abuse and being taken over continued. I was seeing her four times a week and speaking with her on the fifth day, trying to create a sufficiently safe haven for her to express, contain, and understand her terrors. While she typically turned to me for safety, support, and understanding, when the paranoid fears became most intense, she became fearful that I, too, would torture her or attempt to control her for my own purposes. During one poignant moment when she was curled up in a ball on the chair and sobbing, feeling utterly helpless and hopeless in dealing with these terrors, I happened to tilt my rocking chair ever so slightly forward. Startled, she placed her hands up on the wall as if trying to climb to safety. I had a sense of a little girl being physically beaten and having nowhere to turn but to the wall. I calmly described the events that had just occurred and how she appeared to feel so unsafe and terrified. When she was calm, together we spoke about the power of her fears and of their relational origins.

During this particular period, however, her suicidal terror, her impulse to jump to freedom, intensified. Because she was living alone, we agreed, to the relief of both of us, that she needed a hospital to create a sufficiently safe place in which she could experience all of the emergent terrors and not feel all alone, but safe, so as to integrate her previously dissociated affects and memories. As part of this reintegration process, she needed a place, unlike a private office setting, where she could scream out the full intensity of her terror and rage.

> *Comment: Our dyad was serving as an oasis in a sea of dangerous turbulence, and the respect we each had for the initiative of the other allowed Samantha to participate as a partner in our cooperative effort to consider hospitalization. In terms of the incident in the office, Samantha, using her prior lived experience of danger and abuse, predicted my rocking chair movement indicated an incipient attack. Based on my lived experience with her increasing trust in me, I predicted my gentle description would facilitate her calming – which involved repair and restoration of the relationship – even after such a powerful disruption.*

Fortunately, I was able to find a private hospital that at the time had one floor with a psychoanalytically oriented staff. She stayed there for a month and worked with a psychologist who, serendipitously, reminded her of me. The hospital served to provide her with the safety needed for her to experience the full range of her terrifying emotions and memories. She screamed her fear and her rage. She would cower in the corner, sob – and talk. At the hospital she had individual and group treatment, phone sessions with me, and the camaraderie and support of other patients who felt much of the same. All of these supports cocreated a sufficiently safe place, a holding environment (Winnicott, 1965; Slochower, 1996), in which to feel, express, and contain her terrors and rage.

During this period Samantha became terrified of her parents and refused to see them. She had remembered and recognized what had occurred in her family. Toward the end of her stay, she was prepared to see her parents, and she invited them to visit. Her mother, however, declined, ostensibly due to other commitments, and the meeting did not take place. Samantha was enraged, and this time expressed herself more assertively to her mother.

When Samantha was discharged, she was fragile, but stable. The terrors had diminished and we proceeded with our analytic work. One year down the line, she anxiously, yet with a sense of triumph, discontinued her medication. Over the next several years, the terrors subsided and our work took on a more even tone. Samantha dreamed:

I was taking a math class. Realizing that I needed help, I went back to the professor, who was kind and non-judgmental, which reminded me of you.

He spoke to me quietly, calmly, and my panic subsides. I still do not understand how he explains the process of finding the solution, but at least I feel less frustrated and isolated. He does an entire problem for me, from beginning to end on a page; he writes out all the short steps along the way, leaving nothing out. I watch him write – it is very comforting. He tears the page from his pad. When he is done, he hands it to me. Now I feel I have a way to follow, a frame of reference for the next problem I will be given. I leave feeling relieved, less scared, less frustrated.

In Samantha's dream she envisions a protective, idealizing selfobject relationship in which the analyst is calming and knows how to solve the problem, providing a roadmap for the next problem she'll be facing. She easily related these qualities to her experience with her analyst.

Comment: Working cooperatively together with a protective, older male, which made her feel "less isolated," and sharing moments of enlivening experience were evident both in the dream and in the analytic process. Her dream rendering of the professor's skill in meeting her precise needs draws on the child's awe and admiration for the caregiver who knows just what she needs to be successful in carrying out an intention. The affectively laden sense of competence and safety emerging from learning new procedures for dealing with life's problems, in turn, gradually raised the threshold for negative experience and lowered the threshold for positive experience and reduced the potential for panic.

Not working steadily and living alone, Samantha began to feel isolated and in need of more connections with people. She had particularly prized the groups in the hospital where she could just be herself – unlike what had been her usual experience in life. I suggested that she join one of my analytic groups, and she did. Group therapy became a place where she could practice being herself and speak her mind.

The themes of feeling judged, controlled, and imposed upon, as well as distrust of others, all entered the scene at one time or another.

Moreover, she became acutely aware of how she, now identifying with parental attitudes, could become the judgmental, controlling "Swiss–German good girl" who imposes her agenda on others. On a number of occasions, the therapy group became the threatening, problem-ridden family and she wanted out. These issues were reworked time and again. With an increasing sense of agency, of doer doing, and evolving self-delineation and freedom, Samantha increasingly was able to respond empathically and perceptively to others, and her relationships – and our relationship – deepened.

Her relationship with her parents changed dramatically. A joint session with her mother facilitated communication. Samatha spoke far more directly and assertively with her parents. She skillfully extricated herself from her parent's attempts to use her in their power struggles. Once, her mother tried to give her an art object of her father's. Noticing her father wince, Samantha objected that her mother had not asked him, and turned to her father and inquired about his feelings. As she was able to hold her own with them and not feel overwhelmed, she was better able to accept their limitations and to receive what they had to offer. In turn, her parents appeared to become more often directly loving and supportive.

> _Comment_: Samantha was able to help her mother and father reflectively process feelings that, in this instance, averted a possible disruption between her parents when her mother took action that was potentially injurious to her father and that might have evoked a rage reaction. A dynamic systems perspective would predict that as one member of a family changes – in this instance, Samantha – it might alter the family system and lead to change in the other individual family members. In addition, she was increasing her capacity to predict her own reactions as well as those of others – mastering intimacy.

Samantha began to date again. She seemed to have little difficulty in meeting men and in becoming romantically involved. She became more aware, however, of her tendency to rush into passionate sexual relationships with men before she had developed more a fundamental emotional connection. Gradually, as she became less expectant of being controlled and terrorized and, in turn, more willing to risk emotionally exposing herself, her relationships with men deepened.

Comment: Samantha was becoming able to attach in more complex ways: she was less frozen and more affectively present. Using
more balanced sensuality and sexuality, she was now able to forge a
more lasting romantic connection. This contrasted with her previous
attempts to enter into attachments more or less exclusively through
sexual passion. Her balanced sensual/sexual connecting with men,
along with a reduction of anxiety, was more in keeping with social nor-
mative expectations and enabled her to cocreate more easily shared
enlivening experiences.

After four years of analysis, Samantha had improved considerably. She felt
much better about herself, and more alive. Her affective experience was
more available to her and more manageable. Her trust in me had grown
immeasurably, and she was becoming more expressive of affectionate feelings for me. At the end of one session, she inquired at the door if it would
be okay to give me a hug. She said that she was feeling close and wanted to
thank me for hanging in there with her. She initiated the hug; with affection
I received her hug and hugged her back – something that is comfortable for
me when it feels as fitting as it did at this moment. For both of us, this was a
poignant hug that powerfully communicated trust, affection, and gratitude.
I was particularly struck by it, for, as we discussed in the following session,
it was an expression of her trust that neither of us would misinterpret the
hug. It was like a watershed after what she had come through in her previous analysis. Subsequently, upon parting after sessions, Samantha either
extended her hand for a handshake, or wanted to have a brief hug, or else
preferred, especially when she was upset with me, to have no contact at
all. Our routine for parting developed in such a way that she could initiate
whatever form of physical contact occurred to her as fitting and that articulated her feelings. I was convinced that this variable routine broadened
her affective experience, her sense of safety, and the intimate connection
between us. We were moving into what has been called "intersubjective
relatedness" (Benjamin, 1988, 1995; Fosshage, 1997, 2003; Shane, Shane,
and Gales, 1998; Stern, 1985): a realm of relating that requires an expanded
expression of the analyst's subjective experience to create a reciprocal (yet
still asymmetrical) subject-to-subject intimacy.

Comment: Research on the topic of physical touch in psychoanalysis
(summarized in Fosshage, 2000) indicates that hugs initiated by the

patient are most often experienced as therapeutic, while hugs initiated by the analyst can more easily engender distrust. The analyst's responsiveness to the patient's initiative to hug can cocreate an authentic sense of being known, as well as a shared moment of enlivened lived experience.

After four years of analysis, Samantha had the following dream, which provided us with a sweeping view of what had been occurring. The dream was presented in three parts, as follows:

I. A village – It extends up (and down) a slope. It is not a steep slope, but gradual and graceful; it is feminine. It is winter. I am looking down on the village as if on a model train set. I see their roofs; they look like old leather books perched on each house. There are train tracks that wind through the village, unifying and connecting it, making it whole.

There are green pine forests, main streets, central squares, country roads hidden under the snowfall. It is quiet, peaceful, lovely. I know that I am the village as well as hovering above it. It is the landscape of myself.

II. A feeling of fear. I am filled with the kind of terror that sent me to the hospital. It is huge, unmanageable, overwhelming. It is all over me; I feel it on my skin, and inside of me. I am paralyzed with fright. This fear is old, familiar. The village goes into a state of suspended animation. It is frozen and still; there is no movement. The me that is in the village ceases to feel. I have the familiar sensation of fear followed by an absence of feeling.

III. Time has passed like in the telling of the Rip Van Winkle story. There is the feeling of 20 years (but I know it has been more) going by. The village has remained in its state of suspended animation. I have lived without feelings all this time.

There is a thaw; the village comes back to life. The cottages are in the same place but feel as if they have been moved to new locations. The relation of the train tracks to the villages and cottages looks the same when I view it from above, but the me that is *in* the landscape feels different. I am disoriented, but not afraid. I am thankful that the frozen sleep is over. There are icicles melting under the eaves of the cottages; the light falls with a different slant on the landscape.

At the end of the dream I am only in the landscape, no longer above it. I am finding my way through unfamiliar terrain. The thaw has caused patches of earth to appear from under the snow. The landscape is no longer pristine as it was in the beginning of the dream (when it was a model… a model child), but I feel grounded in it; it is much more real and filled with vitality.

We understood the dream as depicting a dramatic story of an ongoing psychological transformation. The Rip Van Winkle sleep of twenty years had begun when Samantha was nineteen: the beginning of adulthood, as she put it, and also the age when she met her former husband, although, as she notes in the dream, she had been asleep longer. Brought up as the model child, she was graceful and feminine, and had achieved some peacefulness, but at the cost of being "wintry" and distant from her own experience ("I know that I am the village as well as hovering above it"). In the analysis Samantha began to reconnect with feeling, encountered terror, and, as in the past, froze to put a stop to it. Gradually, as we understood and helped her work her way through the fear, she began to thaw, to be "within" her experience, and to become more alive.

Over the past five years, Samantha has pursued her writing, including graduate school, and has more and more successfully maintained her focus. Publication of her writing has been the reward that has added reinforcement and incentive. Along the way she shared her writing. I have felt appreciative and affirming of it. As is apparent from her dreams, she is highly capable with images and language. She knew that I wrote and inquired about it. We shared our writings and our experiences of writing. This sharing provided times of mutual recognition, of twinship experience – moments of intimacy involving intersubjective or subject-to-subject relatedness. Here we were clearly one person relating to another with mutual respect, affection, and concern for one another.

Comment: Sharing our writings and our experiences of writing provide us with "moments of meeting" (Stern, et al., 1998), or what we call "shared enlivening moments" (Lichtenberg, Lachmann, and Fosshage, 2016). Included were moments of mutual surprise and admiration.

As the age of forty was closing in, Samantha became quite upset about the prospect of not having children. She was the last hope for her family.

While she felt her parents would be disappointed in her not having children, with my encouraging nudge she spoke with them and discovered, to her surprise, that they were not invested in grandchildren, but in *her* happiness. She developed what was her best romantic relationship up to that point, but the man already had children and did not wish to embark on that path again. Due to a variety of serious setbacks in the man's life, the relationship came to an end.

Subsequently, Samantha and a close male friend began to express loving and sexual feelings for one another. He was in the process of extricating himself from another relationship. His and Samantha's relationship progressed, including sexual intimacy. One day Samantha came in and excitedly said, "Jim, I am finally getting sex and a relationship together." Samantha's announcement of this progress additionally ushered in an increased intimacy in our relationship. As we explored the new experience she was having with a man we were also able to express positive and affectionate feelings for each other. She could do this more easily, for she now felt that the playing field between us was level. It was more person-to-person and, yet, asymmetrical (Aron, 1996).

> *Comment: Over the years of psychoanalytic treatment the tensions between us gradually ameliorated, ruptures were quite quickly repaired, and reflective awareness was far more easily recovered when momentarily lost. In addition, the lowered threshold for positive experience gave rise to a lightness, to a considerable increase in humor and play between us. Our acknowledging the effect of these positive changes on each of us promoted further developments in the areas of sharing moments of enlivened lived experience, heightened affective moments, and enhancing an authentic sense of engaging in the world and of being known. The underlying affective tone was shifting from anxiety and terror to calmness, playfulness, confidence in her creative work, and enlivenment. The anxious states, of course, could be triggered and, yet, recovery was much more rapid.*

Samantha decided to take a high-paying, full-time position in the arts, heading up her own department. She had become more financially conscious and responsible and wanted to have material things for herself. She had built a good reputation for herself and negotiated admirably. In closing, I will present in summary from a recent session with some detailed exchanges that occurred the morning after her first day of work. The context of our having worked for a considerable time together needs to be kept in mind in reading the summary, for analyst and analysand are dealing rather quickly with primary thematic issues as they emerge in the session, currently triggered by her new job. These issues are quite familiar to us and we have mutually developed a reflective awareness, conceptualization, and vocabulary in regard to them. During the session Samantha was clearly struggling with the now long-recognized thematic battle between being herself and being controlled by those around her, now in the guise of corporate structure.

Samantha opens the session by saying, "This is the first full-time job since 1991 and I am stressed." I inquire, "What's the stress?" She responds, "Fear of being trapped." I ask, "In what way?" She describes how she needs to eat every two hours (extensive use of antibiotics had totally dysregulated her system) and does not want to reveal it, for it places her in a weakened position as the head of a department with people she does not know. We discuss how her response to being physically dysregulated on the first day at work is understandably upsetting. Yet, her reaction also appears to resonate with what became her own perfectionism – that is, with attributions based on being "the perfect child." After focusing on various practical alternatives, Samantha ends up poignantly saying that she does not want to be at her new job and wants to go home. I continue to explore: "Any other reasons?" She responds, "It's boring, unsafe, I don't know what I'm doing." She relates it to feeling trapped in school, bored and inhibited. With her freelance jobs, she could be in for six months and then "out of there." In a somewhat pleading tone of not wanting to be forced to do it, she reiterates "boredom, claustrophobia, and complexity of relationships." I emotionally join her and reflect, "Yes, in a freelance situation, you can work six months and then get out of there and you're fine." She says, "Yes, and I could continue to do that. Why should I have to face forced commitment? My commitment to you comes out of desire, need. I love you and, if we have difficulties, we work them out." I respond, "That's a new model, a new way of doing things, in contrast to what it often felt like at home." She answers, "At home I felt driven to be something I'm not. I'm not fully myself. I had to perform perfectly at home." I reiterate a vision of "being" that we both "know" and, yet, she has momentarily lost touch with: "Maybe you don't have to be so perfect at work; maybe you could take some time to absorb, familiarize, get your footing." She picks up the message, "You know I only need a pad and pencil until I figure out what I'm doing." She describes several interactions in which she was honest and "not perfect" and then says, "I feel like killing my father. The perfectionism came from him." And then, with a slightly helpless tone, "I'm disappointed that it's so deep." I respond, "Yeah, that's the way it is. That's what happens when these neural networks get activated." [Neural networks are something that we have discussed in detail]. We discuss again how one has to regain a reflective awareness of a theme and its origins to free oneself from its grip – in this case, the feeling of perfectionist expectations and demands. She is reminded of how, as a girl, she would sneak out of her window onto the roof – to be alone, smoke, and regain her equanimity. I respond, attempting to open up the new avenue: "Yes, there you couldn't solve it in the relationship; now, perhaps you can; perhaps you can just *be*, and then you can be at home wherever you go." She responds with feeling: "That would be wonderful!" There is a reflective pause. And then she exclaims flatly, yet with considerable satisfaction: "You know we did it! Thank you, I can breathe again!"

The theme of perfectionism, of being the model child, along with its underlying anxious affect, had once again been activated. Being quite experienced with this theme by this time, we were able relatively quickly to regain a reflective perspective about it and to reclaim a sense of freedom from the perfect-child self-state. In my responses, I reminded her of an alternative vision, of a way of "being" that had previously been achieved, to which she could now emotionally relate. Confirmation of this momentary success came in the group therapy session, four days later, in which she relayed what had happened and how "happy" she had been since the last session.

Looking back, Samantha and I have traveled a long way together. Development had occurred in all three of the pathways that we are emphasizing in this book: 1) the pathway of human relatedness and intimacy; 2) the pathway of mastering the environment; and 3) the pathway for a healthy body, physiological regulation, and a good mind–body connection. These pathways, while distinct, often intersect. More central to this transformative analytic process was expanded development in intimacy and mastering the environment. Samantha had developed a good–mind body connection throughout her life. During childhood and adolescence she had studied ballet and modern dance, with considerable success. In young adulthood, she decided not to make dance her career, for it had been so totally consuming. Subsequently, she chose musical dance workouts and speed walking for physiological and emotional regulation.

When Samantha entered psychoanalytic treatment, she was "flying high" from being "in love" with her previous analyst, and yet she expressed *an underlying affect tone of anxiety and worry*. After finding her way to extricate herself from her previous analyst/fiancée, we found that her underlying affect tone of anxiety primarily emanated from a frequently and powerfully activated core conflict of subjugation to or rebellion against her parents and their expectations and agendas – the way she was "bred" that Samatha experienced as so incongruous to her "inner integral self."

Her anxiety was about "being enough," about expressing her feelings and needs in the face of parental opposition, about "living up to," defying, or subjugating herself to parental expectations. Her parent's pressure and volatility had fragmented her self-narrative and resulted in an emotional shut-down and frozenness: "My inner self had been squashed and wants out or I will die…I was the perfect child – forget it – I am not the repressed, elegant Swiss–German girl."

Yet, her parents' cultural values, hard work, and success appealed to and resonated with her, stimulated familial pride, and contributed to the formation of her goals and self-esteem. If only her parents had not been so self-focused and forceful with their agenda, and even terrorizing, in their expectations. Feeling heard and understood created a new, desperately needed experience with her previous analyst that was forfeited when her analyst's needs came to the forefront, usurping analytic space.

Samantha and I played out these themes during our work. Think of the rocking chair incident when Samantha, feeling vulnerable and fragile, was traumatically startled and terrified by the slightest movement of my rocking chair. Her father would have screamed at her for feeling so vulnerable and scared. At that moment, I was able to feel her terror and spoke ever so gently and calmly to talk her down from the terrorizing ledge of fear and distrust.

We made our way through episode after episode of terror, of her feeling endangered, unprotected, and all alone. Despite the traumatic imposition of her parents' agenda, Samantha nevertheless was resiliently able to maintain some sense of an authentic self along with a considerable determination to develop and further realize what was experienced as authentic to her. Processing and repairing traumatic ruptures both within and outside the analytic relationship contributed to a growing sense of competence and self-regulation, as well as a sense that others could be helpful rather than just a source of further shame and upset. Our close tracking of her experience, emphasizing affects, meanings, intentions, and goals, contributed to her extricating herself from the parental attributions and to articulating and consolidating a more cohesive narrative of her authentic self, all occurring first and foremost within, but not by any means limited to, the analytic relationship in which she could gradually experience being seen and known by the analyst. Ever so gradually, Samantha began to feel that she could count on me, and that she was no longer alone. She grew in confidence. With determination, she worked hard in her writing and teaching career, eventually becoming recognized and successful.

The affect tone of underlying anxiety receded and was replaced by an increasing affect tone of excitement from feeling like a "doer doing"—a sense of competence in "mastering the environment." The analytic ambiance over time became us "doing" the work together with lightness and humor, and with enjoyment of each other and of her, and our, accomplishments, all of which increased intimacy and satisfaction – the pathways of human relatedness and intimacy and mastering the environment. In the last session presented, this patient/analyst ambiance enabled us to competently and quickly address reflectively, and to rebalance when the old anxiety "will I be enough?" was activated, as it was when she anticipated the new job.

As she continued to consolidate a more cohesive, positive sense of an authentic self – or, in other words, as she became more fully her own person – Samantha gradually desired a fuller relationship in the analysis with the entrance of more of my subjectivity, which was now no longer terrifying to her. Our subsequent experiences of sharing moments of enlivening experience and heightened moments of surprise, humor, and mutual admiration was based on, as she expressed it, "a level playing field." With the increased sharing of our subjective experiences with one another, analysis became one person relating to another (subject-to-subject relating). Now, liking and affection could be mutually experienced and expressed both verbally and through physical touch where sensuality, not sexuality, was in the forefront. Hugs and handshakes, initiated by Samantha, were potent affective communications. Each had a distinctive meaning and fit the occasion, serving to regulate the closeness between us as well as increasing her sense of personal agency, an experience of being a "doer doing." These verbal and physical expressions of affection emanated from a hard-won sense of safety and self-assuredness that stood in contrast to the previous traumatic childhood and analytic transgressions. The sensual/sexual thread (a very important distinction; Lichtenberg, 2008) varied from a softness and tenderness in speaking, in "being with," to a more overt description that highlighted affirmation and mutual feelings of sexual attraction that could now be expressed within an arena of trust and safety. *Humor and playfulness increased and substantially contributed to a patient/analyst ambiance of lightness, enjoyment, and loving connection.* Overall, her originally high threshold for experiencing positive emotions was lowered and her low threshold for negative affects was raised. Over the past year, I realized that we had developed a special greeting when I picked Samantha up in the waiting room early in the morning: I loudly and heartily express "SAMANTHA," and, in resonance, Samantha exclaims "JIM," an ambiance that is emblematic of our mutual enjoyment of each other. The world, self and other, had become safer, enlivened, and enlivening.

References

Aron, L. (1996). *A meeting of minds.* Hillsdale, NJ: The Analytic Press.

Brandchaft, B., Doctors, S., and Sorter, D. (2010). *Toward an emancipatory psychoanalysis.* New York: Routledge, Francis and Taylor Group.

Benjamin, J. (1988). *The bonds of love: Psychoanalysis, feminism, and the problem of domination.* New York: Pantheon Books.

Benjamin, J. (1995). *Like subjects, love objects.* New Haven: Yale University Press.

Bowlby, J. (1973). *Attachment and loss: Volume II: Separation, anxiety and anger.* The International Psycho-Analytical Library, 95:1–429. London: The Hogarth Press and the Institute of Psycho-Analysis.

Fosshage, J. (1997). Listening/experiencing perspectives and the quest for a facilitative responsiveness. In A. Goldberg (Ed.), *Conversations in self psychology: Progress in self psychology*, Vol. 13, pp. 33–55. Hillsdale, NJ: The Analytic Press.

Fosshage, J. (1999). Different forms of intimacy: The Case of Samantha. Presented at The 22nd Annual International Conference on the Psychology of the Self, Toronto, Ontario, Canada.

Fosshage, J. (2000). The meanings of touch in psychoanalysis: A time for reassessment. *Psychoanalytic Inquiry.* 20 (1): 21–43.

Fosshage, J. (2003). Contextualizing self psychology and relational psychoanalysis: Bi-directional influence and proposed syntheses. *Contemporary Psychoanalysis.* 39 (3): 411–448.

Lichtenberg, J. (2008). *Sensuality and sexuality across the divide of shame.* New York, NY: The Analytic Press.

Lichtenberg, J., Lachmann, F., and Fosshage, J. (1996). *The clinical exchange: Technique from the standpoint of self and motivational systems.* Hillsdale, NJ: The Analytic Press.

Lichtenberg, J., Lachmann, F., and Fosshage, J. (2016). *Enlivening the self.* New York, NY: Routledge, Taylor and Francis Group.

Shane, M., Shane, E., and Gales, M. (1998). *Intimate attachments: Toward a new self psychology.* New York: Guilford Press.

Slochower, J. (1996), *Holding and Psychoanalysis.* Hillsdale, NJ: The Analytic Press.

Stern, D. (1985). *The interpersonal world of the infant: A view from psychoanalysis and development.* New York, NY: Basic Books.

Stern, D.N., Sander, L., Nahum, J., Harrison, A., Lyons-Ruth, K., Morgan, A., Bruschweiler-Stern, N., & Tronick, E. (1998). Non-interpretive mechanisms in psychoanalytic therapy: The "something more" than interpretation. *International Journal of Psychoanalysis, 79,* 903–921.

Winnicott, D.W. (1965). *The maturational processes and the facilitating environment: Studies in the theory of emotional development.* New York: International Universities Press.

Summary of Chapters 2 and 3

In Chapters 2 and 3 we present narratives of the successful analysis of two patients who experienced deeply painful struggles with an identity formed in childhood that was incongruent with their sense of themselves as adults. We use the clinical stories of the treatment of Eileen and Samantha to illustrate our experience-based revision or restatement of analytic theory. Rather than sexual or aggressive instinctual drives, we regarded seeking as the spark for the activation of the effects, intentions, and goals of each motivational system. Rather than ego and superego, we describe three developmental pathways for seeking: one to seek human relatedness and intimacy; one to seek mastery of the environment and confidence in one's skills, learning, creativity, and ability to play; and one to seek bodily health and a satisfying appearance. From the beginning of life, values and goals are drawn from the social and ethical context of the individual's daily life. Values emerge from interacting and intersubjective experiences with others. Three-month-old infants are drawn to those who help and avoidant of those who hinder them in achieving their intentions and goals. Information is organized as conscious symbolic and presymbolic sensor-motor narratives and as out-of-direct awareness underlying pervasive affect tones that emerge from the success or failures of each pathway for seeking. A parallel to the underlying affect tone is the ambiance, the tone that emerges between the analysand and patient.

Consequently, the analytic treatment comprises multiple facets; most well-known from the brilliance of Freud is understanding and insight into the nature of influences that have resulted in adaptive and maladaptive trends in identity, expectations, and intentions in each motivational system. The analyses described in Chapters 2 and 3 provide rich details of the patients' traumatic past.

Patient's and analyst's interlocking associations, reveries, and reflections on memories, dreams, and model scenes become recognized sources of discontent and shame, debilitating failed attempts to expose and repair an entrenched maladaptive sense of self. The success that each analytic pair achieves in gaining insight and integrating past experience with present distress and ineffectual approaches to being a doer doing bind analyst and patient as a trusted working pair who share moments of affirmation, twinship, and ideals. This familiar mode of therapeutic process is nicely illustrated in these two clinical stories. All of this achieves well-deserved levels of conscious and preconscious formulation and reflective recognition, as illustrated in Chapter 2 and 3 (see also *The Clinical Exchange* and many other studies and books).

In Chapters 1, 2, and 3, we hope to have illustrated that something more than interpretation and insight is occurring in parallel with the more defined presymbolic and symbolic processes leading to explanation and meaning. A more diffuse generated affect tone emerges in any successful ongoing exploratory treatment as the mutual interplay of patient and therapist forms, consolidates, and changes. We emphasize that we are referring to an ambiance that develops between analyst and analysand. Ideally, we believe that as trust, caring, and mutual understanding increases, positive change will be reflected in the patient's underlying affect tone. Often, however, an analyst's underlying affect tone is vulnerable to a response in kind and picks up on a patient's tendency for irritability, depression, pessimism, denial, provocativeness, seductiveness, and withholding, and the way in which the analyst's own underlying affect tone tendencies coincide. One ambiance will develop if the analyst can sense into the patient's feeling state and share it to a degree, but permits a goal of seeking success in inquiry and change is retained. Or does the analyst get caught up in a countering affect response: anger, defensiveness, shaming, and put-downs often expressed in enactments? Or is goodwill retained and expanded? Is a generalized tone of trust, sensual sharing, and inquiry able to be developed and expanded? If so, the patient's underlying tone of negative affects and pessimism will gradually be modified. Alternatively, if the treatment leads to erotic outlet being resorted to or dominant – in-submission power struggles becoming predominate in the relationship – the patient's underlying affect tone will remain unaffected. The clinical narratives of Chapters 2 and 3 present clear examples of success, with the difficult task for the analyst entering motivation disturbances of each of the three pathways being to be richly involved while maintaining goodwill, a spirit of inquiry, and a sensual connectedness. Developments in the ambiance between them then becomes a vehicle for changes in Eileen's and Samantha's underlying affect tone.

Reflections

We have presented several variants of familiar analytic concepts: seeking is the fundamental spark for being a doer doing feeling, intending, and meeting goals. Three developmental pathways form to seek human relatedness and intimacy; mastery of the environment and confidence in one's learning, skills, and ability to play; and bodily health, physiological regulation, a satisfying appearance, and a good body–mind connection. An underlying generalized affect tone develops that reflects success or failure in seeking in each pathway, and contributes to the individual's disposition, sense of self, and identity. Successful exploratory therapies contribute to modification of the underlying affect tone through interpretation, insight, and empathy, and especially from changes in the ambiance between patient and therapist. Sensuality, a spirit of inquiry, and a sense of power as doer are each a major component in the development of a positive affect tone in the ambiance and in the formation and heightening of goodwill, in and out of treatment.

Chapter 4

Disappointment and disillusion

The distinction between the effect on seeking and disappointment and disillusion that we will present was stimulated by my (JL) discussion of a paper by Mor Shechory-Stahl at the IAPSP meeting in Vancouver 2019. We will present Mor Shechory-Stahl's paper followed by my discussion. This is a series of clinical narratives of brief or lasting disillusion from my years as Resident and Clinical Director at Sheppard-Pratt Hospital and my own analysis.

Disillusion: its negative impact on seeking

Humans seek to fulfill their needs and desires by being a doer doing adapting to the actual world. Infants move toward their approaching mother, open their mouth to be fed, push the nipple out when satisfied, and seek pre-verbal communication and interplay. Throughout life, a person's failure to accomplish their intentions and goals in the actual world leads to disappointment and hopefully to an attempt to modify the approach taken or a search for an alternative fulfillment and success. In addition, humans seek to fulfill their needs and desires by forming an illusion of themselves as a successful doer doing in a fantasy narrative. Infants replace their absent mother by rubbing, cuddling, or hugging a blanket, bottle, or stuffed toy against their body, nose, and mouth (Winnicott's 1953 transitional object). Throughout life, disruptions of an illusion being relied on to fill the gap of a missing resource leads to startle, confusion, and often a period of intention disillusion that frequently paralyzes carrying out intentions.

Introduction

All creatures are born with some capacity to seek to discover what they need and want and to seek to obtain it, removing obstacles if necessary. Humans add to the motivational systems involved in successful seeking a recognition of the meaning of their seeking to their own welfare and the welfare of others. But humans are able to take a hugely important step further with their agency: in the absence of what they seek they can imagine – that is, create in fantasy – an illusion of the desired. With this illusion they can live for periods of time more happily and often more productively. They can be less disappointed and antagonistic. They can sometimes remain on the lookout for the actuality of the sought out if it becomes available while at other times elevating the illusion to be an entity in itself to be clung to. When dealing with an actuality, success in its attainment leads to pride and an incentive to seek for the success, and failure results in disappointment and an incentive to modify and review the effort. When dealing with a significant illusion, success in its maintenance may lead to little incentive to modify or make further effort to pursue a flexible intention and goal. Disruption of a broadly maintained illusion is often traumatic, leading to feelings of disillusion, the cessation of effort, and deep feelings of pessimism, helplessness, confusion, shame, and loss of vitality.

The transference–countertransference activated in psychoanalysis lends itself – we might even say invites – illusion. Who does the patient come to believe her analyst is: the father she never had? The mother whom she wanted to have a deep understanding of her? Who does the analyst come to believe her patient is: a person fully committed to the treatment? A person who has full and deep trust of the analyst's skills and intent? Idealization of this nature provides powerful bonds holding the commitment of each – of analyst to this patient, of patient to this analyst. Disruption of a moderately idealized other generally can be tolerated and discussed. When the illusion is intense, is being clung to desperately, disbelief, especially if abrupt, leads to shock, confusion, and disillusion.

I will present several examples from my residency analytic training and an experience of my own. In addition, I will present papers describing treatment by Dr. Mor Shechory-Stahl and my discussion. I will then broaden the discussion to consider the myths that bind together cultures, religions, and societies.

Similarities, dissimilarities, and blind spots in therapeutic relations

Mor Shechory-Stahl, PhD

But one's own must be learned as well as that which is foreign

Hölderlin

In their choices and lives, people are influenced by dimensions of similarity and dissimilarity or strangeness between themselves and their surroundings. Observation of social groups reveals that communities emerge on the basis of similarity. Usually similarity elicits good feelings, a wish to approach and get to know, to imitate or even to identify, a sense of security and trust in the other. Experiences of dissimilarity, by contrast, are likely to trigger feelings of incomprehension, criticism, insecurity, suspiciousness, and a wish to keep away (Del Rio, 1984). The sociological term *homophilia* (love of the similar) refers to humans' tendency to attach themselves to those who resemble them, those with whom they share beliefs, values, education, etc. Psychoanalytic theory already refers to fear of the different, and the need for closeness to the similar, in Freud's 1919 paper on the "Uncanny," where he discusses the semantics of the German adjective *heimlich* – familiar and intimate – and its opposite *unheimlich*, denoting the uncanny, or strangeness. Freud writes: "the uncanny is that class of a frightening which leads back to what is known of old and long familiar." Self psychology explains this need for similarity and intimacy. Heinz Kohut wrote that one need of the self is the need for "twinship," the need to be in a relationship with a similar person: someone with whom one feels there is a common denominator, who gives a soothing sense of belonging and prevents feelings of nonbelonging and loneliness (Kohut, 1971).

Though much has been written about the therapeutic relationship, on the subject of similarity and dissimilarity as it occurs between therapist and patient and affects their relationship there is hardly any published work at all. Theoreticians of psychoanalysis nevertheless suggested early on how the subjective person and real components of the therapist – such as gender, ethnicity, external appearance, personal history, and psychological elements – affect both transference and countertransference, and currently theoreticians stress the centrality of the therapist's subjectivity in the therapy. But in spite of significant theoretical work in this field, there is a need for more in-depth and specific elaboration of the subjectivity and intersubjectivity emerging from similarities and dissimilarities in the therapeutic dyad.

Intersubjective similarity and intersubjective dissimilarity

Every therapeutic dyad includes interactivity between elements of "intersubjective similarity" and "intersubjective dissimilarity." To an extent, some of these elements are easily identifiable and known to both subjects in the therapeutic dyad – for example: gender, external appearance, religion, profession, and education. Other elements are known to only one of the parties – either the therapist or the patient. And, in addition, there are elements of difference and similarity between patient and therapist that go unidentified and are unknown to both. These latter unknown and unconscious zones are the most susceptible to projections, splitting, and dissociation. The influence of these zones on the therapeutic process is not accessible to analysis, processing, recognition, or understanding unless the therapist undergoes processing and analysis.

When we ask ourselves whether the dimensions of similarity and dissimilarity in the therapeutic dyad may produce blind spots in the therapy, we might assume that dissimilarity, due to the negative feelings it often provokes, is more likely to lead to blind spots. I believe that in cases of similarity the risk of blind spots is even greater. It is particularly high where unprocessed parts of the therapist encounter unprocessed parts of the patient. This is reflected in the following vignette.

Case study

Majda, a young, traditional Muslim, intelligent and impressive, was referred for therapy to my Tel Aviv clinic in Israel. She lived in a Muslim community with her husband and children, was good looking, elegant, and very successful, both professionally and financially, as a lawyer. Majda grew up in a middle-class family and is the oldest of three siblings. She perceives her family as warm and close, yet at an early age she used to take on roles in which she supported the family. Her younger sister was born with cerebral palsy following a complication at birth and Majda has always treated her as no one else in the family has been able to.

She turned to therapy due to anxiety attacks and physical symptoms which, following a long process of medical check-ups, were understood as being mental in origin. Her physical condition and her anxiety almost entirely prevented her from engaging in her work, or from being a dedicated mother and daughter. This functional change also seriously affected her self-perception. While she used to feel capable of taking up any challenge, she was weak now, depressed, dependent, helpless, and scared. She came to therapy wanting to return to her former self.

In therapy, Majda spoke about her relations with her family, her parenting, and about other significant relationships. In all of these, close or more remote, she would somehow zoom in on the people who were in need and come to their help in a total way, whether the support required was emotional, technical, or financial. Majda habitually ignored signs that told her to stop her boundless giving, much like she often ignored the red light in her car when it warned she was running out of fuel: Again and again, she would find herself stuck on the road with an empty tank. Majda had a grandiose, omnipotent perception of herself, denying and refusing to accept herself as a person with needs and limitations. Her family had always treated her as an all-powerful savior, and she conformed to this perception. In our therapeutic work we understood and interpreted the anxiety attacks as both body and mind telling her she was under unreasonable strain. For many years she had been setting aside her own intuitions about her limitations, and, just like her car, she found herself stuck now that her strength was exhausted and her mental "tank" had run dry.

When overnight her anxiety attacks stopped her in her tracks, during therapy she found herself having to rehabilitate and rebuild herself in a more balanced manner, with a self-perception that included split-off and dissociated parts. This involved a process of mourning as she had to come to terms with both physical and mental constraints. Gradually, Majda grew stronger, and became able, both at work and in her personal relationships, to function and focus herself, while also protecting her boundaries and looking after her resources and strength.

The religious and cultural differences between Majda, an Arab–Israeli Muslim woman, and me, a Jewish Israeli woman of European descent, were often present and mentioned in our meetings. In many senses, Majda's life involved a lot of back and forth between her Islamic culture and the local Jewish one. She lived in both worlds in parallel: she was familiar with both cultures, spoke both "languages," and was competent and natural in switching between them. This too was how our therapeutic conversation went. Her great familiarity with and understanding of my Jewish culture enabled her to explain her own language and culture to me in my language. In the course of the therapeutic process and my deepening acquaintance with Majda and her life, I learned about a world view, about family and social relations and norms, in a neighboring and yet remote culture.

Her personality and her culture, as they came through in her stories, and the complexity of her life as a Muslim woman in a Jewish state, impressed me. In one such story she described an intrusive, humiliating security check at the airport on her return from a working trip in Europe. This incident, and ones like it, did not make her angry; she felt only sadness and understanding: "I understand them. The ones who do the terrorism are the Arabs." In spite of the political and security situation, and of the natural human tendency to feel fear of the other and the unfamiliar, she felt sympathy and identification with Israeli–Jewish culture. She sought to raise her children with an openness to the other culture: she created opportunities for them to meet with Jewish people, took them to after-school activities or summer camps with Jews – but she expressed her frustration because in spite of her attempts "they are afraid of Jews." I wondered what about her own fear? What about her anger?

In the countertransference I felt sympathy, closeness, and compassion for her and her people. I felt uneasy about belonging to an occupying nation. I had to contain within myself my feelings of guilt and helplessness regarding the political situation. Time and again we had to keep the political and security situation from entering the clinic. But we felt that in the small bubble of the clinic and our personal encounter we were managing to create a coexistence marked by communication, acceptance, and understanding.

At this point I would like to zoom in on an event which occurred in Majda's past, and which is related to the present discussion as well as the way the therapeutic process evolved. In her twenties, Majda had been present at an horrifying terror attack when two Muslim suicide terrorists – one on either side of her – had blown themselves up. She was surrounded by the bodies of the killed and injured while she herself, miraculously, was unscathed. Soon enraged bystanders moved in on the scene and started yelling "Death to the Arabs!" She observed how a young man near her was identified as an Arab, immediately captured, and taken away. Majda froze. She realized that she would be in danger once they realized she was an

Arab. Thus, from having been in mortal danger due to her own Arab fellow citizens, the danger now, within minutes, was coming from the enraged, violent, Jewish crowd. Rescue teams arriving at the scene asked her to help, but Majda was afraid to open her mouth and reveal her accent. The security forces interpreted her silence as a sign of a panic attack, which attracted more attention and increased her fear and helplessness. As she remembered it, it took a long time until she managed to extricate herself from the scene and escape to the safety of her home. This extremely traumatic event clarifies the impossibility of life within conditions of violent conflict in which there exists a confusion of dangers and identities, and internal chaos suffused with fear of death. Experiencing and witnessing, in therapy, Majda's trauma, confronted me with my own trauma. Many years earlier, I had been present during a terror event and found myself in mortal danger. It was a miracle that I emerged unharmed. This event had a major impact on my life. The terror attacks we had experienced were similar: We both survived them, and they occurred during the same period and in geographic proximity. Two women, two nations, two traumas in a therapeutic space that has to hold the dissimilarity and the similarity as they intermingle, creating an indigestible compound.

While the therapy was making good progress, with Majda growing impressively stronger both physically and mentally, we were coming closer in time to Israel's Memorial Day for the Fallen Soldiers and Victims of Terrorism. Reality entered the clinic when it turned out that our weekly session coincided with the time when the siren would be going off to mark the remembrance services in cemeteries throughout the country. On this day, every year, I attend a ceremony at the graves of close friends who lost their lives. It is an almost sacred day of mourning for me. I mused, to myself, on the coincidence, literally, of Majda's weekly meeting and the ceremony. For the first time since Majda began her therapy, I found myself reflecting on what we knew yet hadn't thought about. I began to feel emotions connected to the strangeness between us and additional meanings concerning the fact that we belong to different peoples who are locked in an ongoing, bloody conflict. These feelings are hard to contain in a relationship marked by the intimacy we had both been trying to build and maintain. So far we had kept such feelings at arm's length. I tried to imagine how it would feel not to go to the annual ceremony and instead be there for Majda at our usual hour. How would that be? What do the sound of the siren and the ceremony mean to her, and what do they mean to me?

Memorial Day brought to the surface a more complete acknowledgment; both of us knew it, but had apparently not thought about it, in Bollas's (1987) terms. I chose to go to the ceremony and make space for my own mourning. I wrote to her that I had to move the meeting, and offered her some alternative times in the same week. Majda replied she was technically unable to make it on any of these times. She also cancelled the two next meetings in the subsequent two weeks, again giving practical reasons. She did not answer my phone calls, and three weeks after Memorial Day she stopped responding to my text messages. For some months I continued trying to contact her, to suggest we should resume contact and pick up the therapy, but she remained silent. And so Memorial Day for the Fallen Soldiers and Victims of Terrorism turned out to be the day on which this therapy came to an end, and with it the personal and intimate coexistence between us.

My world view, personality, and personal and professional values all led me to have an open attitude of acceptance toward Majda and her difference and her dissimilarity. In this therapy, like in others, my own subjectivity and difference were present from the start. I believe that she sought therapy with a Jewish therapist who was different from her in order, among other things, to examine the dynamic she knew so well from her frequent transitions between cultures and languages. Questions of belonging versus being different were part of her intrapsychic world, just as they were part of her everyday reality.

Looking at the earlier-mentioned dimensions, there were many elements of dissimilarity and similarity in the clinic between me and Majda: they marked the therapy and largely affected it. We were from different cultural, ethnic-religious, and linguistic backgrounds. We were alike in being women who combined motherhood with a career. We were situated at the two poles of the Israeli–Palestinian conflict but shared an approach to coexistence, which we tried to achieve when we met in the clinic. We were both women who knew what it meant to devote oneself to the other. Each of us had been through a traumatic experience in which our lives were in danger, and each of us had miraculously survived.

What was the political and social context to our relationship? Something emerged between me and Majda that gave room to dissimilarity, to difference, to social-political tension, and allowed for an attempt to enter a process of healing. Ziv (2012) coined the term "the political third," which represents a joint creation of patient and therapist. What, then, was the "political third" between Majda and me? Ziv also mentioned the constant presence of an ethics of suspicion. In what way did the dialectic of fear in the political-social-national context make itself known in the relations between Majda and me? Majda and my political third included closeness and a wish for healing and reparation, but there was also the fear of death, the fact of our belonging to two peoples between whom there is hate, trauma, and violence, which stayed denied and untouched. Much like in many other aspects of her life, where she denied the constraints of her body and mind, maintaining a grandiose self and an illusive experience of self-competence, Majda felt she could deny the complex social-political context of her life both as a Muslim woman in Israel and in the therapeutic dyad. An additional dialectic that marked the therapeutic discourse is one that both Freud (1919) and Kristeva (1991) mentioned, namely the elusive dynamic of taking an emotional position vis-à-vis the other, which includes both a need to identify with her or him, and a fear, or even rejection, of her or him.

Majda's shifts between cultures and languages served as a way of protecting herself from the experience of being a stranger, which had become linked in her mind to both national and personal trauma. Schecter (1980) theoretically linked trauma and experiences of strangeness. He argued that when an infant encounters trauma, having no other way of dealing with the event, it freezes. Shecter calls this freezing and dissociation in reaction to a traumatic event the "shock of strangeness." Simultaneously, a repertoire of adaptive interpersonal strategies develops. This comes to help in avoiding contact with the terrible experience of strangeness in the infant's contact with himself and with others.

The therapeutic situation at hand included two terror-related traumas and two experiences of cultural-religious strangeness. Majda's and my ability to contain the meaning of these traumas and the resulting experience of psychic strangeness was naturally limited. In this way, an experience of cultural-religious strangeness, similarity in trauma, and psychic strangeness in the meaning of the trauma became entangled.

On Israel's Memorial Day, which closely precedes Independence Day – days during which the Israeli–Palestinian conflict becomes especially prominent on the public agenda – both our psyches enacted the dissociated split-off parts, which we had not seen or felt. Memorial Day confronted us with the need to integrate split-off parts of acceptance and fear, of appreciation and rage, of familiarity and similarity, on the one hand,

and strangeness, on the other. The traumatic event Majda experienced was marked by a dramatic inversion of the roles of enemy and attacker: Those who were supposed to protect her (the Israeli security forces and the bystanders) turned, in her experience, into dangerous attackers themselves. Unconsciously, perhaps, the transformation of the dangerous attacker was reproduced at the precarious moment of Memorial Day, when she became aware of the fear that, from being a person who protected her and was her familiar partner, I might turn into an attacker.

Dissociated and split-off parts, both Majda's and mine, led to something that the therapeutic relationship could not hold. My cancelling the meeting that would have coincided with the Memorial Day siren caused her to feel there was something our relationship could not hold. Why couldn't I meet her on that day? She might have become anxious about what she imagined had happened inside me, or maybe she herself felt incapable of meeting me on such a day. It was too hard to get a sense of our "political third." When it made itself felt in the therapy, the wish to escape arose, maybe in order not to spoil the idyllic experience Majda needed. And so, like in the case of her reaction during the terror attack, when she felt her life was endangered, with me too she reacted with silence. This might have been the result of an unconscious experience of feeling that dangerous emotions might upset a balance of denials to which she had learned to stick, and which continued in our relationship too.

That the therapy came to an abrupt end on a day which connotes the very essence of mourning, the very core of political conflict and of trauma for both Palestinians and Jews alike, is an enactment. Enactment, too, represents a special moment of encounter between therapist and patient, when transference and countertransference processes become blurred and contact between the patient's and the therapist's unconscious worlds occurs. This mutual and shared dissociation is what enactment is about: a split-off self-state of the patient encounters a split-off self-state of the therapist (not-me parts). These dissociated and split-off parts were entailed by the dimensions of similarity and dissimilarity. It was a cultural strangeness and distance in the political-social-religious context that became linked to similarity in the dissociation resulting from parallel traumas, the depth of whose meaning neither one of us could have held.

My own understanding of my dissociative parts and split-off self-states emerged as a result of the sudden ending of the therapy and continued to evolve while writing this paper. I hope that this important therapeutic process can be resumed and completed if and when Majda returns to the therapy, when I can be in touch with those threatening, split-off self-parts. My ability to hold these parts will make movement possible and undo the freezing, so that we can then come to hold together the threatening emotions which in our joint illusion became part of the others, the strangers. A continued process could integrate Majda's denied and split-off parts around the social-political-security experience and other denied and split-off parts in her mind and in her daily life, which were responsible for the anxiety attacks and mental-functional crisis which she initially came for therapy.

Conclusion

Dimensions of similarity and dissimilarity between therapist and patient are present, to different degrees, in every therapeutic dyad, and their impact on the therapist's subjectivity, her therapeutic stance, and the way therapy proceeds requires more attention. Similarity and dissimilarity occur in terms of gender, religion, culture, and profession, as well in biographical and intrapsychic details. Like yin and yang, similarity and dissimilarity entertain relations of opposition and complementarity. One cannot exist without the other: dissimilarity will always include similarity, and similarity always involves difference, which equals separation. The similarity between therapist and patient may lead to blindness to what is different, strange, separate. The dissimilarity between them may prevent them from seeing similarity. At both ends, there is enmeshment and a lack of separateness between the therapist's self and that of the patient. Being able to distinguish between intrapsychic projective elements and actually present ones, in response to the influence of the intersubjective similarity and dissimilarity between therapist and patient, will make it possible to identify what is unconscious and blind and therefore likely to block vital therapeutic processes.

References

Bollas, C. (1987). *The shadow of the object: psychoanalysis of the unthought known*. New York: Columbia University Press.
Del Rio, V.B.Y. (1984). The "real" similarities and differences in the psychoanalytic dyad. *Journal of American Academy of Psychoanalysis*, 12(1): 31–41.

Freud, Z. (1919). *The Uncanny*. Complete Psychological Works of Sigmund Freud. Volume XVII . The Hogarth Press and the Institute of Psycho-Analysis.

Kohut, H. (1971). The analysis of the self – A systematic approach to the psychological treatment of narcissistic personality disorders. *The Psychoanalytic Study of the Child*, Monograph No. 4. New York: International Universities Press.

Kristeva, J. (1991). *Strangers to ourselves*. New York: Columbia University Press.

Schecter, D.E. (1980). Early development roots of anxiety. *Journal of The American Academy of Psychoanalysis*, 8: 539–554.

Winnicott, D.W. (1953). Transitional objects and transitional phenomena – A study of the first not-me possession, *International Journal of Psycho-Analysis*, 34: 89–97.

Ziv, E. (2012). About a stubborn trauma. *Mafteakt: Lexiconial Journal of Political Thought*: 5.

Discussion

Dr. Shechory-Stahl begins with the observation that similarities are the basis for the emergence of social groups. Usually similarity arouses good feelings and approach, and dissimilarity arouses fear and avoidance. I agree, but this is only part of the story. For infants too much repetition of similarity evokes habituation and loss of interest while dissimilarity in the form of variance evokes interest. As for dissimilarity and the uncanny, we have a huge interest, as evidenced by Frankenstein's monster, horror shows, distortion mirrors, Halloween festivities, and the attack of Martians. The human mind, especially in adolescence, seeks avidly to explore the edges of the known and familiar. But what Dr. Shechory-Stahl has us particularly looking at is racial, ethnic, and religious groups who live in close proximity, compete for resources, and have histories of enmity, oppression, and blood-shed: Turks with Kurds and Armenians, southern whites and blacks in the USA, Chinese and Muslims – and, at some point in history, one or another group all over the world.

This is background. The core of this evocative paper is the subject of similarity and dissimilarity as it applies to therapist and patient – an Israeli analyst and a Muslim patient, a "gay" analyst and a "straight" analysand, or a black male analyst and a white female analysand. Dr. Shechory-Stahl asks: do elements of difference and similarity between patient and therapist go unidentified and remain unknown to both? Conscious and unconscious blind spots are, as we know, susceptible to projection, splitting, and dissociation, but she states that what we don't usually think about is that in cases of _similarity_ the risk of blind spots is even greater where unprocessed parts of the therapist encounter unprocessed parts of the patient.

Jumping ahead, the enigma is this: therapist and patient are working together very well. Dissimilarities are brought to the surface and openly

considered. The therapist cancels one session to attend an Israeli ceremony and Majda, the patient, stops contact and never returns – an unex-
plained abrupt end to an apparently successful relationship and treatment.
I will review Majda's unusual pathological pattern in search of a plausible
explanation.

As presented by Mor, Majda was the most compulsive, boundless caregiver I have encountered. As a consequence of the drain on Majda of
her caregiving she was weak, depressed, dependent, helpless, and scared.
Majda would zoom in on people in need and come to their help in an all-
encompassing way – emotionally, technically, or financially. She ignored
her own needs to the extent that frequently she was stuck on the road with
an empty fuel tank.

In terms of motivational systems, her caregiver system had become
totally dominant. Other of her motivational systems – attachment, affiliative, exploratory, aversive, sensual/sexual, and regulation of physiological requirements – had become insignificant in her daily life, a massive
drain on vitality. The adaptive development of the caregiver system begins
with altruistic responses of 18–20-month-old infants to the distress of others. The infants will respond to the distress of their mother and others
with whatever has soothed them – offering a bottle, a gentle pat, a concerned look. At age five, a patient of mine regularly brought her mother
cool compresses for her migraines. Under ordinary conditions of child-
care, child caregiving behavior is balanced with primary caretaking by
parents. Attachment research demonstrates that when children's needs and
distress have been neglected by depressed, absent, or distracted mothers,
8-year-old children will institute a role reversal. The unconscious goal of
caring for the parent is to buttress the parent so that she or he will look
after the child and restore a semblance of an enlivening, loving, supporting
attachment.

A wonderful part of Mor's narrative is the manner in which the two cultures – with their traumatic history – were dealt with. "The religious and
cultural differences between Majda – an Arab Israeli Muslim woman – and
me, a Jewish Israeli woman of European descent – were often present
and mentioned in our meetings." Majda lived in both worlds, and was open
with Mor about her world view and her family and social relations. Their
similarities and differences were personified in the life-threatening terror
events each had encountered. "Two women, two nations, two traumas in
a therapeutic space that has to hold the dissimilarity and the similarity as

they intermingle, creating an indigestible compound." But each worked hard to make it digestible. Majda "felt sympathy and identification with Israeli–Jewish culture." She involved her children with Jewish children, despite which the children felt fear. Mor, for her part, felt sympathy, closeness, and compassion for Majda and guilt and helplessness about belonging to an occupying nation. Despite the political and security situation each lived in, they managed to create a coexistence marked by communication, acceptance, and understanding – an ambiance between them of trust.

And then came the cancelled session so Mor could attend Israeli's Memorial Day for the Fallen Soldiers and Victims of Terrorism – a sacred day of mourning for Mor, with sirens heard throughout the country. Mor wrestled with her decision and turned over in her mind aspects of the countertransference based on the question: What do the sound of the sirens mean to Majda, and what do they mean to me? Mor chose to make space for her own mourning, so we know what the decision meant to her. But what did it mean to Majda that had such decisive consequences?

I suggest we consider Majda's primary pathology. Her extreme compulsive caregiving is, I believe, a dramatic role reversal of conscious giving to unconsciously bring about a restoration of a deep, reliable, loving attachment. I suggest in early life she felt loved and then abandoned. In treatment, she sought from Mor a deep, unbreakable bond of caring. She experienced Mor as saying

Be reassured. I won't let anything stand in the way of my devotion to you. Our differences – religious, cultural, traumas – we talk about, we share, we put aside so I can fill the deep void you bring about in letting your tank go empty.

And then the crunch of reality:

> I am a devoted therapist – but I am not totally a mother completely absorbed with you. I have my own needs and interests. We are indeed the same – that is we have our separate desires; mine are for the Israeli Memorial Day and yours are for nothing to stand in the way of my total preoccupation with you – a preoccupation you give to others and hope desperately to get back from someone.

In other words, I suggest a startled Majda became disillusioned by Mor's cancelling the session for Memorial Day but took away from a well-conducted therapy enough sensitive understanding to carry forward.

Case examples of illusion/disillusion (JL)

During my residency training at the Sheppard and Enoch Pratt Hospital, I (JL) had three experiences that involved a patient's unexpected disruption of an illusion.

Mr. M, a brilliant man in his thirties, had been appointed by President Truman to a high governmental position in health care. Mr. M was ill-prepared for the leadership responsibility, failed, and became psychotically depressed with paranoia ideation. I was the resident in charge of his treatment and we got along well as he unfolded the narrative of his life experience. One day, several months into his hospitalization, we were waiting in the hospital grounds where two men were playing catch with a football. The football got loose and rolled over to where we were. I picked it up and threw it about 20 yards with a spiral – I had been a quarterback. When I looked at Mr. M, I saw he was startled, like he had seen a ghost. He became so agitated that I had an attendant take him back to his ward. Only after a struggle did it become clear what had happened. Mr. M had come to regard me as a twin: an above-average sweet Jewish boy and man. As scholars we were treated as nerds – or even sissies – by the athletes who could bully us whenever they liked. Suddenly, in his eyes I had become one of the bully athletes who had humiliated him. Mr. M's illusion of me in the twinship transference that had sustained the treatment had been disrupted into a traumatic disillusion.

Bonny, a depressed teenager and the only child of a famous family, was hospitalized at Sheppard after a suicide attempt. When I went to see her, she informed me emphatically that her mother had gone to an analyst and it had destroyed her family. She would not talk with me, and that was that. I told her it was my responsibility to see her regularly. For a time, we would sit together in silence. Then I introduced checkers so there was some degree of conviviality between us. I discussed her with Lewis Hill, my brilliant mentor. Lewis said "have her brought to my house and I'll see what I can do." At Lewis's house something totally unexpected happened. On seeing Butch, Lewis's large boxer dog, Bonny was transformed out of her depression and apathy and into an animated, loving playmate with Butch. Bonny asked for, and was granted, visits to Lewis's to play with Butch. One day, several weeks later, Bonny and I were sitting in our usual silence on top of a hill on the hospital grounds. As he frequently did, Butch ran out of the house and headed straight up the hill. Bonny prepared eagerly to receive him, but he came to me – our playful boxing relationship having begun a long time back. Bonny, hands out to receive Butch, looked like she had been hit by a brick. The good – the creative you love and trust – was drawn to the evil – the wrecker of families. An acute moment of disillusion.

I had an attendant take Bonny back to her room. An hour later, to my great surprise, I received a call saying Bonny wanted to see me. When I got to her room, she was sitting in an armchair with wide arms, crying freely for the first time. I sat on the arm of the chair and put my arm around her as she wept. The nurse entered saying she had to take Bonny to dinner. I told her no: she should get Bonny a tray and I would stay with her until she returned. When the nurse returned with the tray, Bonny spoke for the first time: "Now you go home. You should be with your family – your wife and your children." Subsequently, our verbal sessions began.

Mr. E came to Sheppard for a second hospitalization with a schizophrenic episode marked by hearing voices and paranoid thinking. Entering his seclusion room, I quickly sensed his intense hatred and felt an element of physical threat. When I consulted Lewis Hill, who had known Mr. E on his prior hospitalization, Lewis assured me that Mr. E was treatable and agreed to my request to see him with me. I arranged for the two biggest attendants to accompany us. As the four of us entered, Mr. E cowered in the corner, looking a mixture of murderous and frightened. Lewis briefly attempted to reinstate their connection from Mr. E's previous hospitalization. He then turned to the task at hand, saying "You hate him?" Mr. E nodded vigorously. "Is it because he's a Jew?" Intense nod of confirmation. "And you believe the Jews killed Jesus Christ?" Another nod. And then Lewis's challenge to the psychotic illusion: "Who do you think Christ learned all he knew from?" From Mr. E, a look of confusion. "He learned it from the Jews – and this Jew knows something you need to know. Let him teach you." And with that we left the room, a puzzled-looking Mr. E moving out of the corner. About an hour later I had the door opened and spoke to a blank-faced Mr. E: "To get out, stop peeing in the room; call an attendant to take you to the bathroom. Do that and I'll be back tomorrow to tell you the next step." Happily, this "disillusion" with a bigoted moralist illusion about a therapist's religion evolved into a successful therapeutic relationship.

Mrs. T, my first analytic patient, entered treatment depressed. She wanted to have children but so far was unsuccessful. She found it very difficult to talk about or to access and reveal her feelings. She was easily frustrated, and on one occasion was silent for six consecutive sessions. She was a twin, the smaller and less developed at birth. The twin's mother preferred the larger, more developed, easier to feed and handle sister. From the age of four onwards, Mrs. T was determined to win any competition between the sisters – in play and at school. Gradually, her analytic voice became stronger, and she went on to have two children. Her relationship with me became more trusting, with tiny indications of affection. On one occasion I tried to give verbal recognition to an association she had made that suggested mutual affirming between us. I likened the feeling to a rare, golden moment from her childhood when her mother had held her, not her sister, hugging her closely. I chose to repeat her phrasing of "close to her mother's heart" in the language she had used. She erupted in fury, leaving both of us confused and shocked. She yelled "I know it. You are one of the German Jews who looked down on my family, making them feel they were nothing." I later found out that my pronunciation of "heart" was not the Yiddish of her childhood and family but the German of my childhood and school course. It was a moment of disillusion for each of us. I was under the illusion that we had brought into awareness all of the sources of significant negative transferences and were proceeding to a successful ending. Mrs. T, I believe, had long sensed at some levels of awareness a cultural distinction between us, but was proceeding with the illusion that trust in me was earned and goodwill was predominant. So we were both shocked and disrupted: I, that I had triggered such a destructive outrage; and she, that I had revealed myself to be a disdainful bigot. Fortunately, the actual nonillusion strength of our relationship was strong enough that we could recognize and work analytically to resolve our disillusions.

Personal example of illusion/disillusion

My (JL) personal experience with disillusion almost disrupted my career. I had returned from three years as a very young naval officer in the Baltic in WWII to go to medical school to become a psychoanalyst. In my second year of medical school I began analysis four times per week with a young woman who was either a recent graduate or a senior candidate of the Baltimore Washington Psychoanalytic Institute. I felt free to talk about everything: my affection and desire for her, my interest in creativity, my complex family relationships, my social and sexual life. Her interpretations

provided me with considerable insight. Then one day, my freedom to asso-
ciate and my dreams stopped. Finally, I had a dream I related to her. She
took up one element as referring to menstruation. I reacted with angry,
startled screaming: "No! No menstruation!" In her calm voice, she said
"You are right. No menstruation. I am pregnant." The analysis returned to
its prior productiveness, then I received a phone call not to come in – she
was ill, and a week later she died.

After a period of shock and mourning, and after waiting for an opening,
I began analysis with Dr. L, a world-famous training analyst. He seemed
far less responsive, more intellectually aloof, and business-like than my
previous analyst had been. His interpretations interested me. My previous
analyst had been responsive when I cried, as I often did with her, but he
was not. And then, as I was immersed in mourning the death of my beloved
grandfather and my previous analyst, he said "What she did with you was
not analysis; all she did was hold your hand." Many times later I thought
to say "You idiot. If you only held my hand we could get on with this
analysis." But I was too stunned! I went into instant denial and proceeded
as if nothing disturbing had been said. Several weeks went by in which
I heard further insensitive responses to my transference associations. To
complicate the situation, each week I drove from Baltimore to Washington
with three institute classmates, two of whom were also in analysis with my
analyst. They continually praised him as I slunk down in my seat.

This period of denial and distress ended with my having a Kafkaesque
dream of being a crab lying on its back, legs spinning in the air. The crab
must find a way to roll over and right itself or it will die. The meaning
was clear: I had to right myself and get off the couch. As I brought this
up, I was told that if I interrupted the analysis I might as well give up my
training. Feeling completely disillusioned, I quit. Fortunately, the training
committee put me on a leave of absence.

Two years passed and I developed a successful career as half-time
Clinical Coordinator of Sheppard and a half-time private practice of psychotherapy. Sometime in that interval – I think whilst attending a meeting
in Philadelphia – I was standing alone in a room in a museum art gallery
examining a painting when, out of the corner of my eye, I saw a person
entering. It was Dr. L. He circled the room, going past me, and left. I realized he didn't recognize me, and this gave further impetus to my disillusion. Such disillusion often leads to an aversion state, with hurt feelings,
disappointment, anger, and withdrawal. Seemingly out of the blue, Lewis

confronted me, saying "Joe, you are a natural born analyst. All you need is a certificate. Go back and get one." I asked to whom he thought I could go to for analysis. He answered "Dr. A." I said "Dr. A? You said this and this about him." Lewis gave me his stern Prussian look and said "You'd listen to me then, but you won't listen to me now!"

I followed Lewis's advice and it worked out well. Dr. A was a sensitive caring analyst and I was a different analysand. I sensed where he could best help me and, with appreciation, took it in. I sensed that there were issues for which his help was limited. I took the many helpful interpretations and lowered my expectations. I did not unconsciously build up an idealized illusion of a super-brilliant, world-famous analyst who would go beyond my first analysis and repair her loss. After two years, he said I was ready to both end with him and finish my training. Unsaid, but emotionally very important, I could now put aside vestiges of my disillusion with Dr. L.

A final interplay occurred when Dr. L, who had left Baltimore, returned to be on a panel with me and several others. We each gave a fifteen-minute presentation, followed by a five-minute discussion of whatever we wanted to say about our ideas or those of others. Dr. L now appeared elderly and his voice was weak. When it came to my five-minute wrap up, I decided that what he had to say was so important – and in line with my thinking – that I would lay it out for the audience, who had barely heard it. Three weeks later I received a "thank you" note acknowledging what I had done.

Disillusion in the business world: its negative impact on seeking

The affordances of technology in today's world have created super-companies out of start-ups. The "Horatio Alger" opportunity that technology can provide in a business world that sees disruption more as opportunity than threat has helped fuel grandiose illusions for many of today's designers, developers, and young entrepreneurs. The fact is that for every successful billionaire and billion-dollar company that grew seemingly overnight, there are hundreds or even thousands of businesses and business visionaries who met with a much lower level of success – or even abject failure.

Many of these failed visionaries took the lyrical advice of the old song about the ant and the rubber tree plant: "They pick themselves up, dust

themselves off, and start all over again. 'Cause they've got … high hopes."
In these cases, a person retains their capacity to remain, in the words of
Dr. Lichtenberg, "a seeker, seeking" and "a doer, doing."

However, some who fail lack such resilience. When they lose sight of
their dream, they lose sight of themselves. Their illusions of grandeur
become shattered and *all* hopes they might have had get shattered as well.
With no hope, there is no reason to seek. There is no reason to do. This is
the state of disillusion.

As an advisor to business leaders, I've seen many different responses to
both success and failure. To my mind, the saddest, and arguably the most
dangerous, is disillusion.

I submit the stories of Peter and Greg.

The story of Peter

Peter was one of many promising, bright technicians in the dotcom era.
He loved technology and all it could bring to solving business problems.
He loved thinking about how technology could provide quick, scalable
solutions to complex business challenges. He loved puzzles and problem
solving and was highly competitive.

Peter noticed that the more adept he got at solving problems, the dumber
others in the world seemed to be. His confidence in his abilities grew in
proportion to his disdain for authority, tradition, and anything time-tested.
He had no use for his father, who left his mother when Peter and his sister
were quite young. Early in high school, he began to view his mother as an
"unnecessary burden on his freedom" and an "impediment to his mind."
He tolerated high school long enough to graduate and only lasted a semes-
ter in college before he struck out on his own as an entrepreneur special-
izing in designing software for individual businesses. Peter quickly found
clients he could easily help, and he charged a handsome fee in return.
Within a few years he had a full-time client bring him onboard in a crea-
tor/advisor capacity to develop a technologically scaled idea for their new
dotcom product offering. His software solution was so successful that he
and his company were retained to optimize the new technology as a major
selling-point for their company.

Peter was savvy enough to realize he could sell the same technology to
other types of companies in the market with no pre-existing limitations

from his current client. His challenge was that he had a total disdain for marketing ("If the product is so good, why does it need to be marketed?"), and a nasty habit of brow-beating anyone who worked for him ("Why can't they learn to think for themselves? Why do I have to constantly solve their problems?")

I was recommended to Peter as someone who could help him build and grow a company with a strategy that wouldn't require too much of his involvement, time, investment, or leadership.

I quickly determined that Peter's new technology had no competition in the field and could quickly and easily become an industry standard, so I took him on as a client. It didn't take long for me to learn that he had a reputation for being equal parts smart, savvy, and arrogant. In fact, it wouldn't be a stretch to say that people actually liked *not* liking him. Nonetheless, Peter's technology started to become an industry standard, to the point where he was making more money than he had ever made before.

As time went on, he went through employees like water and became more and more disagreeable as his business success increased. It seemed that anytime we talked about how fast the business was growing, Peter could only tell me how he deserved more respect as an entrepreneur and authority from his clientele, his employees, and the marketplace. In spite of his increasing bitterness, his business continued to grow even though he wanted less and less to do with it. It seemed that his favorite refrain was that he was an unappreciated genius who was bigger than one little piece of technology.

Soon it became clear that, based on market conditions and Peter's personal limitations as an owner, it was time to sell his company. Peter was now rich and free from the necessity of operating or owning a business. While he had progressed from being just another technician with one client and no initial personal investment to having millions of dollars and a great lifestyle, he told me he was feeling empty. The captains of his industry wanted nothing to do with him and he couldn't figure out why. He soon began having illicit sexual affairs and spending lavishly on long trips for himself. When I asked him about his plans, he said he didn't have any. When I reminded him that he didn't make enough money on the sale to not have any plans, he said he didn't care. He told me that he made enough not to have to do anything for anyone ever again.

He became listless, bored, and withdrawn. He found himself alone without friends or people who wanted to do business with him. He insisted that he liked it that way. His wife divorced him because of his flagrant infidelity, and he had to sell his house as well as his personal possessions. Peter became a person who had no drive to solve puzzles or problems, or even to discuss ideas.

When we last talked, he told me that he was an unappreciated genius. A one-shot has-been who had a little luck and a little success, but not even close to the degree that his great capabilities deserved because no one listened to him. He also told me he was enjoying smoking pot and recreationally experimenting with hallucinogenic drugs. He had spent what was left of his fortune and lived in a trailer alone, not wanting to talk to anyone. To all who knew him, Peter disappeared.

The story of Greg

Background

Greg, a fifty-year-old man, told me that I came highly recommended from his client. He said he was a life-long learner who was looking forward to improving himself and to achieving his potential, and was optimistic that I could help him with that.

The source of his referral was a business client of mine (a CEO named Mary) who genuinely liked Greg and had let me know that she was worried about his mind due to drastic changes in his ability to perform his job. She had contracted Greg because of his reputation as a highly successful former CFO and CEO with experience in serving in an advisory capacity to new businesses and businesses in transition with new CEOs. He had a reputation as a big-picture strategist. Mary had told me that Greg was increasingly dropping balls on follow-up, missing promised deliverables, and even getting sloppy with his diligence around who received important and sensitive electronic communications. She told me that when she pointed out his changed behavior and asked about these aspects of his performance, he would always apologize with great sincerity and a sense of contrition, yet his performance continued to worsen and became increasingly problematic. She was aware of some challenges he was facing at home and contacted me because she suspected these were the source of his problems at work.

In our very first discussion I asked Greg about how he was doing at work. His response began with "I'd like to tell you about my wife, Patty." So, he did. From the beginning.

"Patricia" grew up in a working-class American family as an only child. She adored her father and liked her mother "well enough." Her father taught high school math. As a little girl she enjoyed music and dancing. In junior high, she joined the school band and changed from a beginning dance studio to one that was more acclaimed and was known for winning high-end dance competitions. Patricia, who now went by "Patty," always had a great affection for her father and viewed her mother as a good house-wife and mother. Her father was handy around the house, always loving to his "pretty Patty," and made time for her no matter what he was doing. Her mother always seemed busy doing housework and the like, and once in a while played the organ in the living room, even though Patty had long ago stopped sitting next to her as her audience of one.

As Patty grew up her affection for her father became stronger, and she grew more distant from her mother, though she remained obedient and polite between her outbursts of petulance, which became more frequent. She became a star dance competitor for her studio and a first chair flautist in the band. She was known as the prettiest girl in school and was very popular. She loved the attention and became increasingly more attentive to her looks and how she presented herself in public.

Her sophomore year, she began dating one of the most popular boys in her school, who excelled in both sports and academics. Greg was hand-some, incredibly optimistic about almost everything, always in a good mood, and adored Patty. Patty and Greg were inseparable. Greg was always at Patty's house for dinner and to do homework. Their many school activi-ties – his sports and her music and dancing – provided ample opportunity for her parents to take posed photos of them together. Patty's mom kept the photos organized in photo albums which became coffee table books in their living room. When company came by, Patty's father would be quick to show off the latest photos to guests and proudly regale them with stories of the latest of his daughter's achievements.

Greg was always the independent one of the two. He seemed to have no fear. He was good at almost everything he tried. Everyone seemed to like him, though he didn't spend much time creating close personal friendships as he was happy spending all his spare time with Patty.

They went to college together and were known as the "perfect high school sweethearts." They often talked about marriage and baby names and planned their future together.

Patty graduated with a teaching degree in music, and Greg earned a bachelor's degree in business. As planned, they married and focused on creating a family. Greg quickly became quite successful in business and Patty enjoyed teaching, but knew she was only biding her time until she got pregnant and could start raising a family.

The first child was a boy they named Geoff. Geoff was followed two years later by a baby sister, Jennifer, who became known as Jenny.

Patty focused all her waking hours on Geoff and Jenny throughout grade school and junior high school. Geoff was a very popular boy who excelled in sports and did well in school. While Greg and Patty doted on both of their children, it was clear to all that Geoff was "Greg's boy" and Jenny was "Patty's little girl." Jenny was enrolled in dance school and Geoff loved playing sports.

The family was described as "perfect" by all who knew them. The children were very well behaved and always impeccably dressed. Both excelled in everything they did, though Geoff was more interested in sports than anything, and Jenny identified with everything dance related. In the meantime, Greg had become a successful entrepreneur. He had built and grown two businesses and sold them both for large sums. He was proud to have taken himself from a working-class kid to a "self-made man" at such a young age. Though he no longer needed to work to earn money, he decided to keep working by accepting requests to advise other companies. He found a great deal of enjoyment in sharing his advice with others based on his own successful business experience. He was always quick to mention to his clients that while building his businesses, he had hardly missed any of his son's games or his daughter's dance recitals. (Greg mentioned this fact to me many times during our conversations, always in the context of how his coworkers admired and commented on it.)

In Geoff's junior year in high school he began struggling with his grades. His demeanor seemed to sour and he spent a lot of time by himself. Greg tried everything to find out what was troubling his son, but to no avail. Finally, during one of their regular father–son talks, Geoff admitted that he didn't feel that he was as smart as everyone else in his class. He also said that he was starting not to like sports anymore because all the other guys seemed much more naturally talented. Greg did everything he could to encourage and help his son become his "old self" again, but things just got worse. Soon, Geoff lost all interest in sports and was barely getting passing grades.

Greg, who boasts about his ability to "compartmentalize things," had recently began consulting with a new CEO named Mary. By both of their accounts he was a great addition to her leadership team, always giving good advice and taking on tough assignments. His demeanor at work was cheery to the point of optimistic, and his ability to sort out problems and offer good solutions was uncanny.

At home, in the meantime, Greg continually tried applying his proven skills to help his son and his family, who seemed all more distant for some reason. Greg saw himself as a highly disciplined person with proven approaches and daily schedules for most everything in his life, from working out to spending time with the family. He strictly adhered to a healthy diet, was diligent about tracking his money, and kept the family on time with their commitments to church and so on. His optimism for how things would turn out remained undiminished, to his mind.

As time went on, his work began to suffer. He was starting to be known by other members of the leadership team as one who doesn't follow through on assignments or pay attention to details. During this time Greg noticed that Patty was withdrawing sexually and had become much less responsive to interaction with him. Besides their children, she seemed to only care about two things: working out and buying expensive clothes, shoes, and jewelry beyond their budget. Greg talked to her often about how her spending was exceeding their monthly income from investments, but to no avail. As Patty seemed to behave more and more in a manner that made no sense to Greg – especially her anger – he kept up with his daily regimen and generally felt pretty good about his "knowing" that things would turn around for them and all would be back to normal soon. But instead, things got worse. Patty didn't want to take any more trips with him and barely went out unless it was for Jenny's dance performances or to work out.

One day, Greg came home from work and Patty told him that Geoff had a doctor's appointment and that Greg needed to take him. Greg, as he usually did, agreed to do so. He asked which doctor and why, but his questions went unanswered. On the day of the appointment, he and Geoff got into Greg's truck and headed to the doctor. Upon parking the car, Greg asked Geoff one more time what the appointment was about. His son looked down and said, "I don't want to be a guy anymore. I'm not as smart as the other guys and I'm not as good in sports as them. I can't compete the way you want me to. I don't think I'm naturally cut out for this. I want to be a girl. Mom knows. This doctor will help me with beginning the process."

Greg was stunned. He asked how long Geoff had been thinking about this. Geoff said "A long time."

After a lengthy pause, Greg realized they may be late for the appointment. Still stunned, he told his son he would always be there for him no matter what, and Greg asked if he could go into the appointment with Geoff. Geoff shrugged an OK.

When Greg got home, he talked to Patty about Geoff. She got angry and began screaming at him in a way that he described as almost noncoherent. Later, as he conveyed this story to me, he said the only thing he could remember was that she said something about everything being his fault. He also told me that she had developed a habit of going to bed without saying good night even when he tried talking to her.

As time went on, Greg's wife became even more removed and seemingly depressed. When she did talk to Greg – which became increasingly rare – she was angry. Greg noticed that his daughter remained mostly friendly to him, but she too seemed to be more self-focused and less family oriented. Individually, both parents continued to do the best they could for their kids, but everything seemed much more perfunctory to Greg, with no sense of love or celebration. He doubled down on being more positive and reflected on how he could return the family to what it once was. He found a psychiatrist through a referral and got Patty and Geoff to agree that they would all see the man.

Two months later, Geoff decided not to see the psychiatrist any longer, and Greg stopped going as well. Patty continued seeing him and increased the frequency of her appointments. A year went by with Patty becoming more angry and distant toward Greg. Geoff began his hormone treatments. All the while, Greg did the best he could to cope, "compartmentalize," and live as "normally as possible" while hoping for everyone else to get back to normal.

At work, Mary told him quite emphatically that they needed him to be better focused as he was functioning at about half of his prior capacity compared to when they hired him. As always, he was surprised and repentant. What he didn't know was that, this time, she was telling him as part of his exit process. He was being fired.

Greg noticed that Patty seemed to be going out more but never told him where she went. She locked him out of her social media and contacts. She became increasingly more private. He suspected an affair, but she denied it and so he disregarded the idea. He started receiving time-stamped photos of his wife's car parked in the psychiatrist's driveway. The sender turned out to be the psychiatrist's ex-wife. It became clear that Patty was having an affair with the psychiatrist Greg himself had introduced her to. He confronted Patty, but she insisted the ex-wife was insanely jealous and just out to hurt her ex any way she could. Greg asked more questions, she but continued to deny any affair. Then she started screaming at him. He was adamant about his memory of her exact words: "You're a failure in disguise as some big success. You've ruined the only son we have. You're not the man of this family. You're not even a man."

Greg realized that despite his optimism and dedication to getting what he wanted, he would never have his "normal" and "exceptional" family again. His perfect world was as shattered as his image of himself.

Greg dutifully kept his appointments with me, though he told me he wasn't sure why. Conversation was almost nonexistent. When he did speak, forced words seemed to suffice in lieu of complete sentences. After a few months, Greg was finally able to converse a bit. He mentioned that he didn't think it was possible to stay married but he couldn't stand the guilt if Patty killed herself. (She apparently had threatened this many times.) He said he also couldn't stand the thought of his kids coming from a broken family. The next time we spoke, I asked him if he'd had any more thoughts about what we had discussed during our previous talk, and he said he had no idea.

He then told me stories about his grandfather and what a great man he was in the war and in postwar America. Greg told me that he remembered crying when his grandfather was dying. When I asked if he cried at the funeral, he said he didn't remember. When I asked if he cried at his own father's funeral, he said no.

I remember during our very first phone conversation, Greg told me that he had only experienced fear three times in his life. The first was when he and his family were nearly hit head-on by a truck. Another time was when he was fired from a job early in his career (the firing, he told me, eventually made him decide to work for himself).

"What was the third time?" I asked.

Greg paused, then stuttered: "It– it's right now. Talking to you."

Conclusion

In Greg's story of himself, Greg became his own version of his ideal hero. And when story of the self-made successful businessman and valued advisor, with the "perfect wife and family," became undeniably untrue, his self-image shattered.

Our understanding of ourselves is the foundational context for everything we know. It is our narrative, or the story we are. It begins early in our development and continues to solidify in the mind as we develop and grow. We spend a great deal of time and effort seeking and working toward validation of our story of self in the world we experience. When we feel that we have found that validation, we see it as reason for us stick to our narrative: "That's my narrative, and I'm sticking to it!" (some of us might add, "Even if it hurts"), We find it difficult to find ourselves in anything counter to our narrative, and therefore instinctively look for ways to negate, deny, ignore, or repress such things.

Schopenhauer wrote, "Why is it for all the mirrors in the world, no one really knows what they look like?" An obvious thought to most who would consider such things is that a mirror is not an image in and of itself. It is merely a reflection – a reflection that is rarely, if ever, viewed objectively by the eye alone, but distorted in some way by the attention and intention of the conscious and subconscious mind looking into the mirror.

Reflection, like beauty, is in the *mind* of the beholder. In this way, life as we know it is more a reflection, like an image in a mirror, than a reality objectively observed and openly responded to. If we were looking into a mirror mounted onto a wall and it instantly and suddenly shattered into a million little pieces, we would be startled to suddenly be seeing only the wall behind it. For an instant our mind would be wondering where the reflection went before we consciously recognized that the mirror is gone. I contend that in that instant we would on some level also be wondering where "we" went.

Let's consider this as a metaphor for what happens as a trigger event for disillusionment. When life doesn't reflect and validate our narrative as we know it (on any level), we are puzzled and left to figure out why. The healthy mind would be able to recover, pick up the pieces, and continue, as Dr. Lichtenberg says, "to be a seeker seeking and a doer, doing." Metaphorically, in such cases, we somehow find a shard of the former whole mirror large enough that we can still see ourselves, but perhaps in a very different way. This requires a shift in our narrative, but the many mechanisms of the mind work to help us come to accept the new image and move on. Sometimes wounded. Sometimes scarred. Sometimes stronger. But still a continuation of a version of a recognizable self, driven and capable to seek and do.

With disillusion there are no shards remaining that are big enough to reflect and validate any aspect of our heretofore self – only a million tiny pieces. When we look into our world to see and validate our familiar selves, there is no trace. Only disillusion.

Disillusion literally means "the freedom of illusion." Our minds need a cage in which to feel free. The boundaries of all we define are determined by how we define ourselves. Who we are, and who we are not – just as boundaries define geometrical shapes, the triangle is defined by the bit inside the lines.

I contend that it is nearly impossible for the mind to understand itself in (or find a connection with) a world that doesn't reflect it in some way. This disconnection can leave a mind untethered and free enough to doubt all it knows – including itself. I contend that a person doubting all their mind knows has far worse consequences than a person not knowing they have a mind.

When there is no longer the necessary cage in which to feel free, there are no boundaries to define us. While losing one's self-created boundaries may sound attractive, and to some is even a goal (from Eastern Mystics to Karl Jung in his later years), it is most often a situation that isn't easily or perhaps even naturally processed by the mind. Boundaries in the mind are as necessary as they are denied, repressed, or battled with. Yet a mind without them is an unbridled power that can be terribly destructive.

Final summary

1. Seeking, in all its complexity, is the spark that activates the feelings, intentions, and goals of a doer doing.
2. Motivation is formed and carried forward in three pathways for seeking and development: the pathway for seeking human relatedness and intimacy; the pathway for seeking mastery of the environment, skills, ability to play, and confidence as a doer doing; and the pathway for bodily health, physical attractiveness, physiological regulation, and a good mind--body connection.

3. Success or failure in adaptive development in each pathway leads to the emergence of an underlying generalized affect tone that contributes to the nature of the individual's disposition, core sense of self, and identity.

4. Change during successful psychoanalysis can be viewed from the bottom up and from the top down. From the bottom up: interpretation and insight into the meaning and impact of developmental factors such as maladaptive attachments and affiliation, and stress or acute trauma, facilitate seeking more successful solutions.

5. From the top down: during psychoanalysis, a shared spirit of inquiry, an immediacy of affective exchange, and an understanding of mutual intentions and goals are relational experiences that sustain the treatment and promote positive problem solving.

6. Less well recognized as a top-down influence is the positive affirming and trusting ambiance that, over time, emerges between analyst and analysand in the intersubjective experience of a successful analysis. During the period of working through, the emergence and continuity of the ambiance not only sustains the treatment, but also has a powerful impact on reversing underlying negative affect tones.

7. Sensuality is the glue that holds together every affectionate pair or group in positive relatedness and sensory experience. The goal of sensuality is a positive pleasurable experience, while the goal of sexuality is orgasmic discharge, very heightened sensation, and relief.

8. Scolding and shaming have a limiting impact on the direction and intensity of seeking, a curb to enthusiasm. Shame, condescension, humiliation, and disdain have a negative effect on the sense of self and identity.

9. Goodwill toward others and one's self and a general sense of well-being present a background that allows an individual to negotiate problematic interpersonal differences and enactments of attempts to achieve unempathic blaming, domination, and/or submission.

10. Disappointment and disillusion as emotional reactions to failure have remarkably different experiential outcomes. Disappointment can trigger seeking an alternate path to success – a demonstration of resilience – while disillusion leads to a collapse of seeking, a feeling of helplessness, inadequacy, and pessimism. Disillusion is a challenge that can occur in psychoanalytic treatment, in relationships, in groups, and in organizations.

Index

adaptive point of view 5–6
addiction 16
affect tone 2, 6–7, 107, 138; altered in
    analysis 4, 6, 8, 34, 39–43, 64, 76–77,
    107; gendered development of 33;
    generalizing influences on 32, 76;
    influenced by shame 44; influenced by
    trauma 39; optimism and 33, 37, 39, 41,
    45, 52; *see also* agentic power; basic
    affection; bodily well-being
affiliative system 15
agentic power: enhanced by analysis 36;
    seeking and exploring as basis of 7
attachment system 14, 15, 17, 19–21, 23,
    35, 43, 121
autism 16
aversive system 15, 22, 27

basic affection: analysis and 36–37;
    sensuality as basis of 7
Beebe, Beatrice 5
Bonny (case study) 123–124
Bowlby, John 5, 8

caregiving system 15
cerebral hemispheres 29–30
Clinical Exchange, The 106
collapse of seeking 4, 8
compassion 29
competence pathway 21–26; affect tone
    and 32–33; physiological regulation

24; power as a doer 23, 25, 28, 30;
    principles of regulation 25; self-
    regulation, sense of 22–23, 25, 38
cultural ideals: masculine heroics 53–54;
    superwoman 54–55

depression 16; maternal 32, 43, 55
developmental pathways 2, 7, 31–32, 38,
    41, 105, 107, 137; as circular process
    35; *see also* competence pathway; good
    health pathway; intimacy pathway
disappointment 4, 8, 109, 138
disillusion *see* illusion/disillusion
disposition/predisposition 34–35, 36, 43
dogs 20
dreams 4, 15
dynamic systems 94
dysphoria 32

ego psychology 4–5
Eileen (case study): affect tone of shame
    67, 69, 70, 72; anxiety 64–65, 67, 68,
    69, 73; aversiveness 71; body shame
    65, 66, 70–71, 72; childhood traumas
    65–66, 67; dreams 70, 71–72, 73, 75;
    fear of exposure 67–68, 69, 70, 72;
    improvements through therapy 74–75;
    intimacy, lack of 67; negative identity
    62, 67, 69–70; previous therapy 68,
    69; relationship insecurities 65, 69, 70;
    transference 72; twinship 62, 74

empathy 29
Enlivening the Self 77
experience 6
exploratory-assertive system 15, 22

fantasy narratives *see* illusion
fractals 8, 63–64, 67
Freud, Sigmund 4, 28, 31, 105, 110,
   116

Gallese, Vittorio 42
good health pathway 26–29; mind–body
   connection 7, 26
goodwill 52–53, 138; *see also*
   psychoanalytic process
Greg (case study) 130–136

Hartmann, Heinz 5
holistic vs. linear experience 29–31
homophilia 110

identity 7–8, 19, 42; shame as 48–55
illusion/disillusion 4, 8, 108, 109,
   127–128, 138; *see also* Bonny; Greg;
   JL; Majda; Mr. E; Mr. M; Mrs. T;
   narratives of self; Peter
infant relations: caregivers 12, 17, 18–19,
   20–21, 22–23, 24–25, 26, 28, 29, 30, 33,
   38, 93; father–infant dyad 11; mother–
   infant dyad 9–11, 12, 18, 19–20, 24, 28,
   30, 34, 37–38, 108; object relations
   10–11, 22, 24, 28, 33; surrounding
   affects 33; trauma 116
instinctual drives 2, 4, 105
intimacy pathway 18–21; attachment
   19–20, 21, 22, 23, 25; communication
   20–21, 38

Jung, Carl 137

Klein, Melanie 31
Kohut, Heinz 5, 8, 44, 110
Kris, Ernst 5
Kristeva, Julia 116

Lachmann, Frank 5
language 20–21; cerebral hemispheres and
   29–30; "Motherese" 20
linear experience *see* holistic vs. linear
   experience
Loewenstein, Rudolph 5

Mahler, Margaret 31
Majda (case study): anxiety attacks 112,
   118; boundless giving 112, 121, 122;
   breaking off of therapy 115, 117, 121,
   122; enactment 117; family history
   111–112; grandiose self-perception 112,
   116; Islamic and Jewish cultures
   112–113, 115, 116, 121; political third
   116, 117; similarity/dissimilarity
   114–115, 117, 120, 122–123;
   strangeness 116, 117; terror attack
   trauma 114, 115, 116, 117, 121;
   transference/countertransference 113,
   117, 122
Morrison, Andrew 44
motivational systems 2–3, 7, 8; seeking
   as impetus for 9, 14–15, 105, 107,
   137; *see also* affiliative system;
   attachment system; aversive system;
   caregiving system; exploratory-assertive
   system; regulation of physiological
   requirements; sensual-sexual system
Mr. E (case study) 124
Mr. M (case study) 123
Mrs. T (case study) 124–125

narcissism 5, 44
Narrative and Meaning 38
narratives of self 136–137; *see also*
   illusion/disillustion

Oedipal period 25, 33, 44–45

pain 9, 13, 26, 27
Panksepp, Jaak 41, 42
Peter (case study) 128–130
Psychoanalysis and Motivation 1

psychoanalytic process: associative/ interpretive process 3, 6, 8, 39, 77, 138; enactment 117; goodwill 52–53, 106; illusion 109; political third 115; presymbolic ambiance 4, 6, 7, 8, 40–42, 76–77, 105, 106, 107, 138; relational experience 77, 138; similarity/dissimilarity 110–111, 118, 120; subjectivity of therapist 110–111; transference–countertransference 4, 39, 88, 109, 110; twinship 106; *see also case studies*
PTSD 54, 55

Rapaport-Klein Study Group 5
regulation of physiological requirements 15
resilience 4, 17, 77, 128
Rochat, Magali J. 42
Roth, Philip 7, 9

Samantha (case study): affect tones 78, 79, 80, 85, 91, 98, 101, 102; attribution of transference 87–88; career 88–89, 98–100; developmental pathways 100, 102; dissociation 83, 89, 90, 91, 92; dreams 82, 85, 86, 89–90, 90–91, 93, 96–97; family conflict 84, 85; group therapy 93, 100; hospitalization 92; intersubjective relatedness 95–96, 97, 102–103; medication 80, 91, 92; parental disapproval 82, 90–91; parental expectations 79–80, 82, 83–84, 98, 99–100, 101; parental relations improved 94; physical and sexual abuse 86; previous therapy 79–80; romantic relations 94–95, 98; selfobject transference 80, 88, 93; suicidal

impulses 79, 82, 91; traumatic memories 90; twinship 97
Schecter, David E. 116
Schopenhauer, Arthur 136
seeking 2–3, 7, 8, 35; analysis of 35–36; exploring limits 123; as fundamental spark 8–9, 15–16, 76; identifying needs and wants 12; planning for needs and wants 12; positive and negative feedback 16–17; stimuli, seeking of 9–12, *see also* infant relations; understanding needs and wants 9, 12; validity of authorities 17–18
selfobject 5, 56
self-sameness 62–64
sensual-sexual system 15, 25–26, 27–29, 138; affect tone and 32, 41; compassion and 29; empathy and 29; Freud and 31; shame and 45–47; transitional objects 28
shame 7, 25–26; cultural ideals and 53–55; identity and 48–52, 138; inhibitor of interest 43–44, 138; reverberating circuit of shame 47–48; sensuality/sexuality and 45–47; treating in therapy 56–57
similarity/dissimilarity 110, 120
Stern, Daniel 5, 41, 42

topographic theory 4
twinship 8, 21, 29, 62, 74, 97, 106, 110, 123

Ullman, Chana 54
uncanny 110, 120
unconscious 4

Winnicott, Donald 5, 13–14, 18, 20, 23, 24, 30, 92, 108

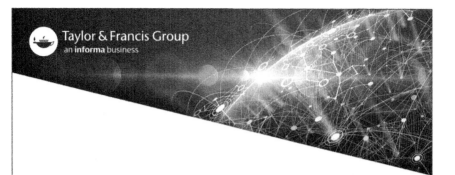